SIX DITCHES

Six Ditches

DEBORAH D. DELBRIDGE

First Printing, 2025 - CovenantBridge Publishing

ISBN: 9798986218342

Copy-editing: Cindy Delbridge Hale

Unless otherwise indicated, Bible quotations are taken from
The New King James Vision of the Bible, Copyright 1979,
1980, 1982 by Thomas Nelson, Inc.

Contents

	Introduction	1
1	Understanding the Human Psyche	3
2	Glitches and Ditches	19
3	The Childhood Branding Ditch	29
4	The Comfort Zone Ditch	40
5	The Blame-Shifting Ditch	57
6	The Depression Ditch	73
7	The Surrender Ditch	92
8	The Shame Ditch	102
9	Our New Identity	120

Introduction

On April 8, 2025, I asked God if He had a teaching for me to help people that are struggling in life. I immediately heard in my spirit, "Six Ditches."

I went to my computer and opened a new Word document. Within a minute or so, I had written down six wrong mindsets that can sabotage our life. When I finished typing one, the next one came to mind, until I realized I had six of them. It felt like a Holy Spirit download. (Of course, there are other wrong mindsets that hinder, delay, or abort our success, but the ones mentioned in this book are the ones that I felt the Holy Spirit wanted me to highlight.)

After I had them written down, I asked God why we are calling them *ditches*. I then envisioned a person in a three to four-foot-deep ditch trying to get out.

If someone is stuck in a deep pit, it would be almost impossible for them to get out by themselves. A pit is deeper than a ditch. It may be hard to get out of a ditch by yourself, but it is possible. It just takes some work. Likewise, the six sabotaging mindsets discussed in this book can be difficult get out of, but it is possible if you develop the skill and strength to do it.

Most people that are stuck in a wrong mindset will not recognize or acknowledge it. Afterall, no one wants to be labeled.

There are several reasons why a person can get stuck in a rut, or metaphorical ditch. They may be *knees deep* in one ditch and waist high in another, meaning they may have multiple issues going on at the same time.

Psychology tells us that our beliefs and our behaviors are driven from our subconscious mind, not our conscious mind. We want to believe we are just having bad luck, but we may not understand that our circumstances could be the result of a wrong mindset. Repeating self-sabotaging beliefs could limit our success and we may not be aware that we are restricting our advancement. This book will highlight some of those subconscious ditches and teach the reader how to get out of them.

Chapter 1

Understanding the Human Psyche

Before we dive into the six psychological ditches, it's important to first understand how our mind works. If you have read any of my other books, you would know I usually teach on the subconscious mind towards the beginning of the book. I do this because it's important to understand that our beliefs and behaviors aren't driven from our conscious mind. What we believe and embrace in our subconscious mind propels our thoughts and actions. Most people are not aware of some of the wrong mindsets that reside within them because their origin is in the hidden place of our heart, our subconscious mind.

A vast majority of Christians would embrace the concept that mankind is a three-part being. We are a spirit. We have a soul. And we live in a body. That definition has been around for decades and has been taught in most spirit-filled Bible schools. Our soul contains our mind, will, emotions, intellect, memory, and creativity.

The phrase subconscious mind isn't in the Bible. It is a psychological term, and it isn't discussed very much in Christian teaching. Christian scholars and pastors don't deny that the subconscious mind exists, they just haven't known how to define it since that term is not in the Bible. The Bible does teach us about the subconscious mind which will be discussed in this chapter. But, for the most part, the Bible uses terms like heart, mind, soul, and spirit to describe the different parts of our human psyche. Oftentimes, when the Bible uses the term heart, it is talking about our subconscious mind. Other times, it seems the terms heart, soul, mind, and spirit are almost used interchangeably, and it is up to the reader to determine the context of what is being taught.

When we accept Jesus in our heart, the Holy Spirit comes and resides in our human spirit. When we are born-again, we become a type of new species because we now have the spirit of God living in us.

2 Corinthians 5:17 says, *"Therefore, if anyone is in Christ, he is a new creation; old things have passed away; behold all things have become new."* We become a new spiritual force on the Earth. As children of God, we carry spiritual authority as sons and daughters of God.

However, very few Christians throughout history have tapped into the spiritual authority that God has endued us with. It wasn't their fault. They operated in the knowledge they had. Spiritual knowledge and understanding have increased significantly since the dark ages. Our generation has the capacity to walk as sons and daughter of God in a much greater dimension than believers before us because we have so much more teaching and revelational knowledge available to us.

We need to get a fresh revelation that God dwells within us. We are not mere men. We are a royal priesthood that was chosen for such a time as this to be in God's end-time army. Each of us has been hand-picked and equipped to carry out specific duties and assignments for God.

It can be confusing for new Christians. They hear verses like 2 Corinthians 5:17 where it says we have been made brand new, and they think there may be something wrong with them. While some addictions and bad habits may have fallen away when they accepted Jesus in their heart, they still have some negative thoughts and behaviors. For some people, it may seem like a contradiction. Are they clean and righteous or do they need to battle their sin nature?

The core of who we are is changed and made new. We now have divinity living in us. Divinity lives in our spirit. However, our soul, which is comprised of our conscious mind and our subconscious mind, still has a carnal nature.

We have been made righteous, so why do we still think and act ungodly? Our soul still has a carnal, Adamic nature that we need to "renew to the word of God" (in Christian terms, Romans 12:2) or clean up and educate (in worldly terms). Romans 12:2 says, *"And do not be conformed to this world but be transformed by the renewing of your mind, that you may prove what is that good and acceptable and perfect will of God."*

We need to renew both our conscious mind and our subconscious mind. Renewing our mind isn't just memorizing a handful of Bible verses. Yes, we need to get God's word in us, but we also need to root out our sinful and self-sabotaging thoughts and behaviors.

Our Subconscious Mind

It was mentioned in the introduction, but it is vital that we understand it. Our beliefs, behaviors, and true motives are driven from our subconscious mind. Psychology teaches this but the Bible also agrees with it.

While the Bible doesn't use the term *subconscious mind*, there is a verse in the Bible that defines the two sections of our soul. Hebrews 4:12 reads, *"For the word of God is living and powerful, and sharper than a two-edged sword, piercing even the division between soul and spirit, and of joints and marrow, and is a discerner of the thoughts and intents of the heart."*

Before I dissect this verse, I want to comment on the first part of this scripture. It says the word of God is "living and powerful." When we read the Bible, new revelations and insights can spring forth. The Holy Spirit can highlight a scripture that we have read a hundred times. He can breathe new life on it and cause us to see it in a slightly different way.

When Martin Luther read "the just shall live by faith" in the Bible, suddenly a metaphorical lightbulb turned on. He had a fresh revelation that people are saved by faith and not works. In 1517, he accidentally started the Protestant movement when he posted his observations and objections on the door of the Catholic Church.

Even in the last hundred years, the church has gained insights and revelations that earlier Christians didn't have. Our spiritual understanding has increased with each new generation and revelational knowledge has come into the church. We now stand on the shoulders of the healing revival preachers that brought the church a new understanding that it's God's will to heal and restore. We stand on the shoulders of the Word of Faith teachers who taught us the importance of faith and standing on the Word.

The Holy Spirit can not only illuminate truths He wants to church to understand, He can also give personal instruction through the word. When we are synced up to the voice of the Holy Spirit, He will direct our steps. He may prompt us to read a verse a second time to draw our attention to it. Then, we may read a post on social media that touches on the subject. We may see a billboard or hear a lyric in a song that mentions the topic. God can use all kinds of ways to get our attention about an issue. We can go back and reread that verse God was trying to highlight to us, and He gives us a new understanding of it. God can give us guidance on how to handle a specific situation. The word of God is living and powerful and God uses the scriptures to lead and guide us every day.

Back in the mid-to-late 90's, when God was teaching me about *diseases of the soul*, the Holy Spirit spoke to me as I was reading Hebrews 12:4. As I was reading the verse one day, I sensed the Holy Spirit prompting me to examine the conjunctive phrases in the verse. Then, the Holy Spirit told me to put the conjunctive phrases into two columns. The conjunctions I am referring to are the "and" phrases in the second half of the verse. They read, "piercing even the division between "soul and spirit", and of "joints and marrow", and is a discerner of the "thoughts and intents" of the heart." When I did, a lightbulb flipped on in me. The Holy Spirit illuminated to me that the first column references our conscious mind, and the second column refers to our subconscious mind.

Conscious Mind		Subconscious Mind
Soul	and	Spirit
Joints	and	Marrow
Thoughts	and	Intents

Let's look at the first column. The conscious mind is where we think and reason. The Bible's metaphor of a body part describes it as joint because the conscious mind is where thoughts are joined together. It is where we reason, where we plan, where we create. The conscious mind is where we connect information, form opinions, organize conclusions, and judge situations. We join together our education with our creativity and think up new ideas, procedures, and strategies. That first column tells us that our conscious mind is where our soul joins our thoughts together.

I find it interesting that the writer of Hebrews used the body part joint when describing our soul. Not only is a joint the place that joins together two things, but a joint in the human body also has a range of motion. As you bend your elbow, your elbow will have different positions. Likewise, your soul sometimes has different positions. At different seasons of our lives, we may have different positions and perspectives. We all filter our thinking through our opinions and biases. Well, those filters may be diverse depending on the season we are in and the circumstances we are facing.

That is also the beauty of the word of God being living and powerful. Two pastors may preach the same verse in different ways, with unique angles. One perspective may not be better or more accurate than the other, however, they teach it from a different angle and highlight different nuances. Those pastors can teach the same tithing verse, but each one is slightly different because the pastors approach it from a distinctive angle according to their personality and how the Holy Spirit flows through them. The different angles are part of the range of motion that their souls contribute to their sermons. The Holy Spirit can use our experiences and personalities to flow through us to offer nuances and insights according to His will.

In fact, this verse is a perfect example of that. How the Holy Spirit illuminated it to me is different than how He would have others teach it. They may highlight the double-edged sword aspect of the verse or some other revelation. But with me, He wanted to show me an insight with the *and* conjunctions. This conscious mind and subconscious mind teaching doesn't nullify or supersede other teachings of the verse. It just approaches it from a different angle. It is part of the manifold wisdom of God. God can give different people revelational downloads that highlight verses in different ways. It doesn't make one teaching right and the other wrong. God is just emphasizing different things in different teachings.

The second column (spirit, marrow, intent) describes our subconscious mind. To reiterate, psychology tells us that our beliefs, behaviors, and true motives are driven from our subconscious mind. The word *intent* is another word for *motive*. So, it appears that the Bible and psychology agree that true motives are originated in our subconscious mind. We may reason and rationalize our beliefs and behaviors in our conscious mind, but our true motives and intents are housed in our subconscious mind.

What is marrow? Marrow is the dark, pasty substance inside of bones. It is hidden and not visible. I think it is interesting that the Holy Spirit inspired the writer of Hebrews to use these two body parts (joints and marrow) to describe something that he didn't fully understand at the time.

Marrow is the part of the body where red blood cells are produced. Red blood cells carry oxygen to every part of the body. The blood that is created in the marrow is the life force of the entire body. What is made in the hidden part of the body is what brings life to every organ, limb, and capillary. Likewise, what is produced in the most hidden place of our soul, our subconscious mind, is what creates and drives our beliefs and behaviors and can be witnessed in our words, thoughts, and actions.

The marrow is also where our immunity is strengthened. Our immunity fights sickness and disease, and it is what keeps us healthy. Naturally speaking, when there is disease in the bone marrow, it makes the body weak, sick, and frail. When our immunity is compromised and weak, it shows outwardly, and our poor health is evident for others to see. Likewise, when there is sickness and disease in our subconscious mind, our behavior becomes sickly and it's evident for others to see.

And lastly, the marrow is where blood platelets are produced. Blood platelets assist in blood clotting, so we don't bleed to death when we are injured. I find this fascinating because our subconscious mind also has types of emotional blood platelets. We have emotional defense mechanisms like denial, repression, compartmentalization, and others that shield us when we can't handle the full emotional impact of a situation. They stop our emotional bleeding until we can process the psychological trauma in our life.

Very few people have any knowledge of the subconscious mind. Most people don't know that the elements in their subconscious mind really do shape their lives. Two people can go through the exact same traumatic situation. One person regresses and wallows in trauma, while the other can succeed and thrive in life. Of course, a person's personality has a bearing on how emotional trauma affects them. However, what a person has residing in their subconscious mind determines how they react and function. The decisions that are made, the beliefs that are embraced, and the actions that are taken are all rooted in what a person has in their subconscious mind.

Yes, we can attempt to make conscious decisions about our attitudes and actions after an offense or emotionally traumatic event. We may tell ourselves one thing in our mind, but ultimately, our attitudes and actions will track with what we believe in our heart. In other words, when we let our guard down, our actions will obey what has been branded and blueprinted in our subconscious mind.

Can we really reprogram our subconscious mind? The answer is yes, but it is not easy. It's difficult because we can't see what resides in the innermost part of our soul. We may be able to see the evidence of it by our words and actions, but we can't see the roots.

A Computer

We can get a better understanding of the human psyche if we use the analogy of a computer. Our spirit is like a motherboard. Our subconscious mind is like a hard drive. Our conscious mind is like a monitor. And words are like a keyboard.

Motherboard

A motherboard, in its simplest definition, is a circuit board inside a computer that stores electrical components and helps them communicate. It is the essence, the heart, of the computer. The functions of a motherboard are to: 1) Manage data flow, 2) Conserve resources, 3) Optimize power distribution, 4) Drive communication, 5) Enhance performance, 6) Improve reliability, and 7) Enable productivity.

Isn't it interesting that these are the things that the Holy Spirit will help us with when we are submitted to Him. When we accept Jesus in our heart, the Holy Spirit takes residence in our human spirit, metaphorically, our motherboard. He determines our capacity. He enhances our performance. He causes us to be more reliable. He assists us with our productivity and He drives communication. He will lead and guide us from our spirit.

Hard Drive

A hard drive is a data storage device. We can't see with our natural eyes what is on a hard drive just like we can't see what is in our subconscious mind. A hard drive stores all our data, programming, pictures, and files. A hard drive stores the files and programs we want but it also stores the junk files we don't want. We can have viruses and glitches on our hard drive just like

we can have junk files, viruses, and glitches in our subconscious mind.

Monitor

A monitor allows us to see some of the programs
we have stored on our hard drive. We can access programs, documents, and pictures. We can create, strate-
gize, and work out solutions. Well, that is what we do
in our conscious mind. A monitor is the workspace of a
computer, and our conscious mind is the workspace of
our psyche.

A monitor can view all the videos and articles on the
the internet. That content is not downloaded on the
hard drive. Likewise, we can see sermons, and teachings we agree with but that doesn't mean that information and complete understanding is downloaded to
our subconscious mind. We may have heard dozens or
hundreds of healing sermons but that doesn't mean
that context is resident in our subconscious mind. True
faith is what we believe in our heart, our subconscious
mind, not what we agree with in our conscious mind.

Keyboard

Neuroscience tells us that we can train our brain.
We can reprogram wrong beliefs and behaviors that
may reside in our subconscious mind. Our conscious
mind is the gateway to reprograming our subconscious

mind. Just like we would use the keyboard and monitor to reprogram a computer hard drive, we can use our words and conscious mind to reprogram our subconscious mind.

Words can reprogram us. The Bible tells us in Romans 10:17 that *"faith comes by hearing and hearing by the word of God."* The word of God, whether that be the written word (logos, the Bible) or the Holy Spirit's spoken word (Rhema), can reprogram our subconscious mind. It can change our identity and change what we believe about ourselves.

What is in Our Subconscious Mind?

- Our Faith
- Our Hopes (Rhema Promises, Impartations, & Aspirations)
- Our Identity (Personality, Character, Memories, & Biases)
- Our Comfort Zones and Subconscious Limitations
- Our Fears, Insecurities, & Emotional Wounds
- Our Emotional Defense Mechanisms
- Our Soul Iniquities/Diseases of the Soul (Spots)
- Our Autopilot, Repeating Glitches (Wrinkles)

I'm not going to give an exhaustive description of each of these things that reside in our subconscious mind. I discuss these things in some of my other books. But some of them are key to breaking wrong mindsets and negative behavior patterns.

Our identity has everything to do with our success in life. What we believe about ourselves will determine who we are. It sets the trajectory for our lives.

Diseases of the Soul are propensities or bents towards certain types of sin. They are our pet sins, our blind spots. They are in our subconscious mind and a person may or may not be aware that they have that character trait. Most people have between two to six of them. Some are more common than others but all of us have pride since it was sired into the bloodline at the fall of man. We may have different degrees of it but none of us are pride free.

Diseases of the soul are like cancer inside our soul. Just like there are different types of cancer, there are different types of soul iniquities. Like cancer, they can go undetected for years before their damage is discovered. They can grow and metastasize without us even knowing that they are silently killing aspects of our life. They can subtly influence our beliefs and behaviors and can sabotage our relationships, finances, careers, and destinies.

They are: 1) pride, 2) fear, 3) unforgiveness/offense, 4) jealousy/envy, 5) rebellion, 6) religious pride, 7) prejudice/hatred, 8) weak willpower/lack of discipline, 9) sexual sins, addictions, and fetishes, 10) idolatry, 11) greed/selfish ambition, and 12) negative, critical, or judgmental mindset.

A more comprehensive study of them can be found in my books, *Blind Spots and Wrinkles.* and *Diseases of the Soul.* These books give a more thorough teaching on soul iniquities, and there is a chapter for each of the 12 soul strongholds listed above. The books discuss several ways each of the disease of the soul can manifest in our behavior so diagnosing them in our life is easier. These soul iniquities are our *spots*.

In this book, I want to focus on our *wrinkles*, our autopilot, repeating glitches that show up in our thought and behavior patterns. To go back to the computer analogy, our soul iniquities (*diseases of the soul*) are like computer viruses, and our negative repeating behaviors are like computer glitches. We will discuss glitches in the next chapter.

Chapter 2

Glitches and Ditches

A glitch is defined as a mistake or irregularity. Do you remember in the first Matrix movie when Neo saw a black cat walk by the doorway? He then saw the exact same thing happen again. He was told that when he saw something repeat itself that there was a glitch in the Matrix and to beware of it. In the movie, when someone experiences a déjà vu happening, it was a mistake in the Matrix A.I. system.

In the context of this book, a glitch is a repeating behavior. For those of us that are old enough to remember vinyl records, when there was a scratch on the record, it caused the same line to repeat over and over again.

Believe it or not, most of us have autopilot type behaviors that we repeat even though those actions are either sinful or self-sabotaging. These glitches (scratches, lines, folds, wrinkles) in our subconscious mind can get triggered when we encounter a situation, emotion, or feeling we have had in the past. As a result, we just repeat the belief or behavior in almost an autopilot manner.

Glitches are our *broken record* behavior patterns. To use the computer analogy, they are a line of programming code that we obey as a habit.

If you look at the section entitled, *What's in Our Subconscious Mind* in the last chapter, you will see that everyone one of these things listed can have auto response beliefs or behaviors.

On the positive side, our faith, hope, and identity (personality) can have good autopilot behavior responses. Certainly, evidence that we have faith in our subconscious mind is that our actions line up with what we believe. That's why the Bible tells us that *"faith without works is dead."* (James 2:14-26)

If our actions don't line up with what we think we are standing in faith for, it is possible that we may not have authentic faith. We may have hope in our subconscious mind and mental agreement in our conscious mind.

I won't be doing a deep dive into personality temperament types in this book, but our personality absolutely can influence our auto responses to situations when they are triggered. Based on the Myers Briggs Type Indicator (MBTI), I am an ESFP. As an ESFP, I am an optimist. My autopilot response is to always look for the silver lining. In a crisis, I don't jump into a fearful response, and I don't assume the worst-case scenarios.

When an autopilot response is negative, those are the wrinkles, the scratch on the record repeating patterns, we want to get rid of. Our comfort zones, subconscious self-imposed limitations, fears, emotional wounds, and emotional defense mechanism can all have hair trigger reactions to situations.

When it comes to *diseases of the soul*, the only way we know we have them is either the Holy Spirit reveals it to us or common manifestations of them show up in our thoughts and behaviors. The manifestations of our *spots* (soul iniquities) are our *wrinkles*. A common sign we have a stronghold of unforgiveness is we get our feelings hurt easily. That knee-jerk reaction to get wounded easily is a negative repeating autopilot response. It is a wrinkle (manifestation). Another example is a person with a strong root of jealousy often diverts attention away from the person they are jealous of. It isn't something they do consciously. They often do it without knowing they are doing it. If the person you are threatened by is getting public praise or attention, a jealous person will say or do something to get the attention off of them. I have observed this happening on a handful of occasions and the jealous person was usually oblivious to what they were doing. These behaviors are usually knee-jerk actions that may not even be noticed or recognized when they happen. Like programming code, they happen behind the scenes. The programming runs without people noticing what is happening, including the jealous person.

Renegade Patterns

Not all wrinkles have their origin deep within the subconscious mind. Sometimes, they are just learned behaviors that were never corrected.

I noticed a behavior pattern in a friend of mine that I have known for about 20 years. When she called a family member and asked them for something, if they didn't agree to it, she cried like a child. I noticed this behavior on more than one occasion. It was a pattern for her. She didn't cry like an over emotional adult. She literally resembled a two-year-old child crying when she didn't get her way. She had big crocodile tears. She looked and sounded like she was an adult impersonating a child. And what happened? Her family members caved and gave her what she wanted. Obviously, that behavior was never corrected as a child and it carried over into adulthood.

I called her out on it when I saw that it was a pattern. She worked on it and corrected it. For her, recognizing the pattern was enough to help her correct it.

Using emotion to manipulate people is a common behavior that many people have. They cry or use anger to get their way. Most of the time, emotional manipulation is not recognized so the person doesn't correct their behavior.

Beliefs and Behaviors from Emotional Trauma

When we go through traumatic events, we can embrace beliefs that impact the rest of our lives. Those beliefs can get imbedded in our subconscious mind and affect how we respond to people and situations.

Recently, I was at a friend's house with my dog. My dog hates to be left alone, so I try to bring him on errands that would accommodate a dog. My dog is very cute, and he is used to people going out of the way to pet him and show him attention.

I noticed my friend was being kind of mean to my dog. Her tone was harsh for no reason. He was trying to please her, but he didn't know what he did wrong. While there, I remembered that in the past she was a little harsh towards him. I knew she wasn't afraid of dogs because she had watched her granddaughter's dog.

I said, "Wow, you don't like dogs."

Much to my surprise, she said, "The only dog I have ever liked or cared about was my dog, Shasha." That surprised me. I have known this woman for several years and up to that moment, I didn't know she disliked dogs.

When I got home, I thought about it. I believe that by rejecting all dogs, it was her way of showing love and loyalty to the dog she lost. She probably said to herself, "I will never love another dog like I loved her." That love for her dog and rejection of other dogs was something she believed at the time. That belief went from her head to her heart, her subconscious mind, and it became a programming code. Her autopilot reaction is to dislike dogs because of the emotional trauma of losing her dog Shasha.

Traumatic events can not only write coding in our beliefs, but it can also program our behavior. I noticed a recurring pattern in another friend of mine that I have known for more than 20 years. When her security gets shaken, she turns mean.

When she was 18 years old, after her mother passed away, she was asked to leave her home because she wasn't getting along with her older sister's boyfriend. She had nowhere to go. She didn't know how to survive on her own. She reacted in a very hostile way. She said the meanest, most hurtful things she could, to her sister at the time. Instead of trying to be levelheaded and work through the conflict, she lashed out. The situation reminded me of a mountain lion when its paw is caught in a trap. That mountain lion lashes out trying to hurt those around it.

Over the years, I noticed that behavior repeating. When her housing situation was threatened, she lashed out and she turned aggressive towards the person she felt was causing the disturbance. Even when the reason for moving had nothing to do with her personally, she still got overly hostile. In one scenario, the person was selling the house and everyone had to move out. In another situation, the person she was renting a room from was moving and everyone had to move. It was like the new situation triggered the old feelings of hurt and her programming kicked in and she became mean.

It is not uncommon for people to have destructive beliefs or behaviors simply because those actions and attitudes have been their *normal*. They never reflected on their actions or chose to see the error of their ways, so those wrinkles of programming manifested when specific triggers happened.

Neuroscience

Neuroscience tells us that streams of beliefs and patterns of behaviors are established pathways in our mind. There are so many pathways that it only makes sense that we have ones that are not beneficial for us.

But thank God, neuroscience tells us we can train our brain and replace negative pathways with new positive ones. The biggest problem is most of our negative beliefs and behaviors go unchecked and unchallenged. They are rarely diagnosed. They are usually not understood so they are not dealt with properly.

A neuroscience instructor who was conducting a training I attended, called our patterns of behavior *pathways in the brain.* In my mind, I envisioned the *pathways in the brain* like a complex freeway system.

The last time I was in Dallas, I was completely amazed by the complexity of all the highways, byways, overpasses, and offramps in the downtown Dallas area. It was a mess. Even with my navigational app on my phone, I still took wrong exits and ended up on streets I didn't want to be on. I immediately drew a parallel between the Dallas freeway system and the neuroscientist's *pathways in the brain.* If we think of our patterns of thoughts and behaviors like a giant roadway complex, we can understand how we can keep taking the wrong offramps of negative conclusions or behaviors.

I'm sure we have all been deep in thought as we were driving and we drove somewhere we didn't intend to go. I know I have done it. After I moved one time, there were a few times when I drove into my old tract. My mind was on autopilot, and it took me to my old house. There have been numerous times when I had planned to stop by the store or gas station before going home.

But because I was deep in thought, my autopilot programming took me home instead.

The same can be true of our thought patterns and negative behaviors. We take the offramps we are used to, even if it means we end up at destinations that weren't intended. They are our *normal*. And we are often blind to the fact that we need to establish a new *normal*.

Some wrong patterns can be adjusted by recognizing the triggers and making a choice to respond in a different way. Other default behaviors may be harder to correct but diagnosing them is the first step.

How do we establish a new mental pathway? We take the new pathway enough times, until it becomes our autopilot behavior. It's a conscious choice to react differently in our mind or with our actions. It may feel like we are off-roading. But the more we drive over that dirt road, the more established that road becomes. Metaphorically, a little dirt road can become a four-lane highway if we travel it enough times. That is how we change our *normal*. We form new habits.

We can't change behaviors we don't recognize. We need to see that they are destructive or sabotaging. If there are painful events that helped birth them, then certainly, emotionally process it, so you can get that area of your heart healed.

We need to guard against the mindset that says, "that's just the way I am." Or "It's just one of my personality quirks." All of us need to "renew our minds" as it says in Romans 12:2. We don't get a *free pass* for our carnality, even if those beliefs and behavior patterns are comfortable for us.

Our wrong patterns of beliefs and our autopilot behaviors can cause us to end up in a ditch in our journey of life. They can stop our forward momentum and even alter the trajectory of our life. Sometimes, it really is the little things that can cause our downfall.

So, take an inventory of yourself. 1 Corinthians 10:12 says, *"Therefore, let him who thinks he stands take heed lest he fall."* What does taking heed mean? It means pay attention to, recognize, and acknowledge. Metaphorically, we need to watch where we are going so, we don't take a misstep and fall into a ditch. If we notice we overreact to a situation, investigate why. What offramps are you taking that are self-sabotaging?

Chapter 3

The Childhood Branding Ditch

According to www.parentingstyles.com, "The formative years in children is between zero and eight years old when the brain and neurobiological development are the fastest after birth. What happens to a child in these years can affect their physical development, mental development, and success in life."

How a child is treated and what behaviors they witness are important. And what is spoken to the child is extremely important. The words spoken to them affect their identity. Identity-shaping words can brand them for life. A child's sense of who they are and what they are supposed to be is shaped in those early years.

If a child is loved and made to feel special, they will value themselves later in life. They usually won't tolerate abusive relationships as an adult, if they were made to feel valued as a child. Their sense of value and worth are formed in their subconscious mind at an early age.

I grew up the youngest of seven children in our house. There was so much activity and mayhem that it really just felt like I was a spectator. I have memories of me just quietly watching arguments, roughhousing, and observing my siblings interact with each other. My earliest memories were always of my mother trying to do things that would please my overbearing and controlling father. It was chaotic. I remember at 5:00 pm, the kids would run around the house and close the windows because when my father got home, he seemed to always yell. The windows had to be closed so the neighbors wouldn't hear him yelling. We expected him to yell at my mother, so we shut all the windows.

I wasn't made to feel special or valued. In fact, on my 12th birthday, everyone forgot it was my birthday.

Bless my mother's heart. She never wanted to show partiality to any one child so she would always say,

"I love all my children equally." I don't remember any words of affirmation towards me spoken by my parents. It may have happened, but I just don't remember any. I don't remember any, "You're smart." "You're pretty" or "I love you" comments that were spoken directly to me.

Not only did I not have positive affirmations, I had negative *identity shaping words* spoken over me. I grew up in the 70's. Back then, everyone had to be thin, super tan, and have blond hair in order to be considered as pretty. I had red hair, super white skin with orange freckles, and I was kind of thick. I was not a cute little kid. In fact, one time when the kids on the street where choosing partners for a game, a boy name Bobby said, "I don't want to be partnered with you, you're ugly."

I didn't think I was attractive, but I didn't know I was ugly. But after that, I went and looked in the mirror, and he was right. I was ugly. Thank goodness, I grew out of some of that ugliness in High School but that labeling stays with us and affects our confidence.

Identity-Shaping Words

A friend of mine was in a major car accident with his mother when he was seven or eight years old. He was in a coma for three weeks and he ended up missing months of school. He had three older brothers who used to call him "dumb" and "stupid" while he was healing from his head injury. They used to tease him that he had "brain damage."

Those identity-shaping words stuck with him. Even though the brain can often heal itself by rewiring around the damaged areas, he still embraced what his brothers called him. As a result of living with that internal label, he has never tried to excel in a career. He has had the same job all his life. When it comes to figuring out electronic devices, there is absolutely nothing wrong with him. He is better at it than me. However, when there is a contract that needs to be signed or drafted, it is like a shield comes up and he won't even try to figure it out. He will defer it to a brother or another friend. I don't know why he is comfortable figuring out complex electronic devices, but he won't even attempt to read a contract. There is nothing wrong with his reading skills. He reads books. But he is intimidated by contracts and anything he believes is above his knowledge level. He has a subconscious block in that area because he believes the words that were spoken over him as a child.

Years ago, a friend mentioned to me that there was a cousin of hers who was called "Baby." That wasn't her legal name but everyone in her immediately family called her that. As my friend was reflecting on the behavior of "Baby" she said it was true. She said that girl acted like a baby in many situations in her life.

I recently had a conversation with a teenager, and I asked her about something. She said, "I can't, I'm lazy."

I then remembered her grandmother called her lazy quite often. She embraced that identity-shaping label and became lazier as a result.

Another family I know calls toddlers and young children in their family "Chunky." With that label, there is no surprise that those kids are overweight.

Even when something is said in jest, the words can stick. Identity-shaping words are important at any age, but they are especially damaging in childhood.

Positive Words

I remember when my daughter was very young. I kept telling her she was "smart" and "pretty." At first, there were a handful of times when she disagreed with me and said she wasn't. But then, she stopped challenging me when I said it. It's almost as if she just accepted it. When she was three and four years old, her knowledge of dinosaurs was beyond most adults. She knew the names of dozens of species and she could pronounce their names. Even when I was looking at a dinosaur name in a book, I still couldn't articulate the names of many of them. Yet, they rolled off my daughter's tongue like she was a paleontologist.

One day when I was picking my daughter up from kindergarten, her teacher ran up to tell me how good Katie was reading in class that day. She said Katie's reading skills were much more advanced than most kindergarteners. She complimented me on teaching her how to read at home.

Well, the truth was, I didn't teach her. She learned it on her own. She picked it up by watching some educational cartoons and teaching herself. I didn't even know she could read, much less, be the strongest reader in her class.

What we say to a child can easily brand their identity. I told Katie she was "smart" so she did what smart kids do. She learned because she believed she was capable. It wasn't until years later that she challenged me with her being smart. She had some difficulties with math, so she embraced the mindset that she had average intelligence. However, all through elementary school, her reading and comprehension skills were two to three years above her grade level.

Proverbs 18:21 says, *"Death and life are in the power of the tongue, and those who love it will eat its fruit."* We must be very careful about what we say to others, especially children. We need to speak *life* over people. We need to speak positive, affirming, uplifting, and hopeful words so we can help them be as successful as possible. Remember from our computer analogy that the keyboard, words, are what programs the subconscious mind.

Our Identity

You are who you think you are, or you become it. That is another way of saying, *"For as he thinks in his heart, so is he."* (Proverbs 23:7a)

Even if we believe a negative descriptive word about ourselves, that lie will eventually become true. Our behavior will line up with what we believe about ourselves.

If we think we are fat, we will become fat. If we think we are a failure, we will become a failure. If we believe we are lazy, we will become lazy. If we believe we are weak, we will become weak. Our behavior will line up with what we believe about ourselves.

This is such an important truth for people to understand. If we don't believe we are valuable and worthy of respect, that will be communicated through our words, expressions, and actions. Soon, others will pick up on it and they will treat us the way we expect to be treated. We may get upset that people are disrespecting us or treating us like a doormat. But unfortunately, oftentimes, we are the ones putting out that vibe.

I'm sure most of us have seen shows where someone has slapped a sign on someone else's back without them knowing it. A piece of paper with tape with the words "kick me" or some other humorous word or phrase was taped to the person's back. We may not have actual paper attached to our back, but we carry the labels we believe about ourselves. Certainly, there are times when people treat us wrong, and make incorrect assumptions about us. But most of the time, people treat us the way we project ourselves to be. They pick up on signals about who we are by our persona, attitudes, and actions.

Assess Yourself

Most people I know have had traumatic experiences from their childhood. Trauma isn't just caused by physical or sexual abuse. Emotional abuse can damage a child in a way that cuts deeper than physical abuse. A child's identity, sense of worth, sense of acceptance, their ability to love and to be loved, are all at stake. Parents, siblings, teachers, neighbors, friends, and classmates can all influence the identity of an innocent child.

Here is an exercise. Take a moment to reflect on your own childhood. At the beginning of this chapter, I shared some details about the environment that I grew up in. Take a half hour and journal your childhood experiences. By writing it out, it will help you remember some of the hurtful or dysfunctional experiences you had.

I know some schools of psychology, spend months or years deep diving into childhood experiences. While having some reflection is good. I am not someone who thinks we need to spend months discovering our *inner child*. Identify and recognize sources of trauma and negative emotional branding experiences, but don't camp out there. The danger of spending too much energy looking for ways you were wounded is, you could cultivate a victim mentality. You may embrace a posture of blame-shifting, rather than focusing on positive changes you can make now to change the trajectory of your life.

How do you discover hidden experiences that may have affected your identity? Ask yourself some questions and reflect.

· What nicknames did you have?
· What did your siblings or classmates say about you?
· Did your parents make you feel special and loved?
· Were you ever rejected or teased by other kids?
· Was there something about yourself that others made fun of?
· Did a teacher ever make you feel stupid?
· Were you physically or sexually abused?
· Do you feel guilty or ashamed of anything that happened as a child?
· Were you ever labeled as ugly, clumsy, hyper, slow, weird, or annoying?

After you have recognized identity-shaping words from your past, look in the mirror, and verbally tell yourself the opposite. If you were told that you were ugly, look in the mirror and tell yourself that you are beautiful. Even if you don't believe it, still do it. There is something that happens when your ears hear identity-shaping words. You can reshape your identity and change how you view yourself.

Change that neurological pathway in your brain. No, you are not stupid. Challenge yourself to do something intellectually difficult. No, you are not lazy. Make yourself conquer a project you have been procrastinating on doing. Stop living the lies that people have spoken over you. You are the captain of your life. Other people don't get to navigate your ship!

The Healer

Absolutely, there are things we can do to correct wrong identity-shaping words spoken over us as well as the hurts and abuses from childhood. But let's not forgot that God can heal our hearts better than psychology and neuroscience.

Psalms 147:3 says, *"He heals the brokenhearted and binds up their wounds."* The more time we spend in communion with God, the stronger we get emotionally. God can reach into those crevasses of our heart and heal our old wounds. The Holy Spirit can whisper new identity-shaping words to us and cause us to embrace those identity-shaping words rather than the negative ones. If we didn't have affirmations as a child or we didn't have stability, God can restore those damaged areas as well. Lean into Him. Give Him your heart and allow Him to heal it.

Chapter 4

The Comfort Zone Ditch

We all have comfort zones in our subconscious mind. Those comfort zones create boundaries that we subconsciously stay in. We may not even be aware that we place self-imposed limitations on ourselves to stay within our comfort zones. Those boundaries are merged into our identity and they are used in how we describe and view ourselves. We give ourselves labels. We give ourselves limits in our finances, relationships, careers, and intellectual abilities.

If a woman had dysfunctional parents who controlled each other through manipulation, intimidation, control, or passive-aggressive behavior, she will probably date a guy who possessed some of those negative traits. It would feel normal to her, and she wouldn't see anything wrong with it. If an emotionally healthy man tried to date her, she would probably brush him off and say, "We didn't have chemistry," "He is boring," or "We just aren't a good fit." What made him wrong for her was he didn't have the negative behavior traits that she was used to. He was outside of her comfort zone.

If a person was raised in a very conservative, stoic, and dogmatic church then that would be their *normal*, their comfort zone. It would feel strange and even wrong for them to attend a charismatic, full-gospel, Pentecostal church. They would challenge the theology even though the basic tenants of the faith are the same. They would probably criticize the music and the preaching, claiming it was too emotional. They would find things that *bugged* them because the church service wasn't what they were used to.

Another example would be if a factory worker has a chance at a promotion to a supervisor position, but they turn it down. He knows that the new position would involve communicating with management and even have some public speaking requirements. That line worker would love the pay raise and even the prestige of the position but their fear of giving presentations and communicating with management causes them to take a step back. With practice that factory worker could have been an excellent supervisor with good communication skills. But they limited themselves because the position felt uncomfortable for them.

We make decisions all the time based on our comfort zones. We limit ourselves and we may even spiritualize it by saying, "I don't have peace about it." We fail to recognize that it wasn't God who said "no," it was our subconscious fear of stepping out of our comfort zones. We think the "no" in our gut was from the Holy Spirit, when in reality, it was our subconscious limitations that said "no."

There is a reason why big companies often hire high-paid salespeople from other industries rather than hiring from within the company. It is easier to train a person in a new product or teach them a new industry, than to instill in them how to make high commissions. That salesperson from another industry may have a learning curve, but they will typically feel comfortable with the demands of the position and with the income potential.

If we took a long-time employee of a company that made $50,000 a year and promoted them to the sale position, they probably wouldn't excel in that position. That employee may jump at the opportunity since most sales reps for the company make over $100,000 a year. That promoted employee may make $60,000 or $70,000 a year in the sale position but their internal *glass ceiling* will usually prevent them from making $100,000. They will most likely be the lowest commission earning salesperson on the team and it won't be anything they are consciously doing. They won't understand why they aren't excelling, and they would probably make excuses for the gap in pay.

There is hope for that long-term employee. They can absolutely make higher commissions if they work on changing their subconscious limitations.

Listening to preaching that teaches that God wants you financially blessed can help break those self-imposing income limitations. Also, rehearsing affirmations about success and money will help too. You may feel foolish, but speaking identity-shaping words over yourself can help break the financial limitations you may have residing in your subconscious mind.

A Poverty Mentality

We can have comfort zones in most areas of our lives. However, I want to highlight our financial comfort zones because they have a huge bearing on our success in life.

If you went to church in the 90's, most likely you heard the term *poverty mentality* preached from the pulpit. It was used a lot in the tithes and offerings teachings. It was taught that a person with a *poverty mentality* holds on to money too tightly. They hoard money and live in fear that they aren't going to have enough money for a rainy day. And while that definition is true, it goes a little deeper than that. There are typically other psychological factors that play into it. A *poverty mentality* can exist not only when a person hoards money, but when they overspend money as well. Both types of people have a subconscious blueprint command in them that says, "I need money" and I will address both in this section.

The Hoarders

It was common for people who lived through *The Great Depression* to hoard money and possessions for the rest of their lives. They understood seasons of lack and they didn't want to ever to be in that situation again. They saved things that could have a use later. They didn't waste money knowing that a little bit of money in a hard time could make all the difference in the world.

That *"save, save, save, don't waste, waste, waste"* mindset may have been passed down to the children and grandchildren of the Depression era people. While some of the descendants followed the beliefs of their parents and grandparents, others didn't. Most children and grandchildren just rolled their eyes and even joked about their grandparents' hoarding habits.

When I was in high school, my best friend's grand-mother went through the Depression, and she was a hoarder. I used to laugh at the impersonation my friend did of her grandmother. Her grandmother would tell her, "Eat the black bananas, they are like honey." Her grandmother had the same box of frozen donuts in her freezer for years. If people came over, she would take out a few of those frozen donuts and serve them to her guests.

I'm sure many of those reading this have had similar experiences with their relatives that went through hard times. Many of you have heard how they *"walked five miles in the snow."*

I haven't known very many *penny-pinchers* in my life. But one example stands out that I want to refer-ence.

A young Christian woman that rented a room from us years ago was a *cheapskate*. At first, I just thought she was frugal, which is an admirable quality. However, the longer I knew her, I discovered it was a bigger issue than her just not being wasteful with money.

After she sold her condo and had over $100,000 in the bank, she still wouldn't spend money. One morn-ing several of us went on an outing. We decided to stop and have lunch at a coffee shop afterward. It was al-ready determined that we would all pay for our own lunches. When it came time to order, she only ordered a scoop of ice cream. I asked her privately why she was only getting ice cream because I assumed she was hungry. She said, "because it costs $1.29." I suggested she get the special lunch of soup, salad, soda, and half of sandwich for only $6.99. I mentioned that it was a great value, but she refused. She wouldn't spend the $5 extra bucks to have a real lunch. I was shocked. She had $100,000 in the bank and she wouldn't treat herself to lunch! I then asked her when was the last time she had ordered a drink in a restaurant. She said, "never." She "only ordered water because it was free."

For her, the blueprinting of money hoarding came from her parents and how she was raised. Both of her parents were very thrifty, and they ingrained that branding into her. Frugal was her comfort zone. She wouldn't feel right spending money on herself because it would feel too wasteful.

The Spenders

I have met several people that have had money management issues. I'm sure most of us know people in that category. The causes of it can vary among the people.

One friend of mine used to be terrible with money. She was on a fixed income and when she got paid, she would go on a spending spree and then not have enough to pay her bills. To her, having money gave her a sense of freedom, so spending it gave her a sense of liberation. That issue corrected itself as she matured when she felt the pressure of not spending it wisely.

My sister Stephanie, who passed away in 2001, was a compulsive shopper. She was an educated and successful woman, yet she had problems managing her finances. When her life became too grim to face, she would escape into her world of shopping. She was an idealist and optimistic and shopping was an escape from her current reality.

Giving gifts and receiving them was her *love language*. She showed love by giving gifts, and she felt love by receiving them. Shopping was therapeutic for her. Not because it represented freedom, but because it represented love. Buying gifts for herself made her feel loved. It was an esteem builder and made her feel valuable. Buying things was like God giving her little presents and showing her love. Her money issue wasn't rooted in a *poverty mentality*. It was an imbalance in her belief structure. Her internal glitch wasn't "I need money," it was "I need love."

The third example I am going to share, I am going to go into a little more detail because it demonstrates how a *poverty mentality* can attach itself to a person's identity.

My brother Ken (who passed away in 2021) had money management issues, as well. Over the years, he had borrowed several thousands of dollars from me. He was smart but lazy. He had the mental capacity to be successful. But his laziness and procrastination prevented him from getting the proper licensing he needed, and it sabotaged most job opportunities.

In the last ten years of his life, any money he received, he sent the majority of it to his friends in the Philippines. There were three women that were scamming him out of money, and he willingly supported these women. Giving to them gave his life a sense of purpose. It was his community. It met an intrinsic need in him to be needed and wanted. He would send money to them a few times a week and then he wouldn't have money to support himself. He came to me several times a week to borrow money for vodka, Black & Mild Cigars, or calling cards. He was an alcoholic and if he didn't drink, he would literally get sick.

Through his words and actions, it was easy to recognize that he believed money was evil. One time I told him, "You think money is evil and those that have it are evil."

He paused and looked confused, then said, "No, I don't." Yet in all his conversations and his frequent *soap box* rants, he would say just that in so many words. Because he gave away all his money, he made comments that those that don't give away all their money were greedy and selfish.

He formed a very ugly view of pastors. If a pastor didn't live below the poverty line, he was quick to label them as a false teacher and he condemned them to hell. He seethed with anger and proclaimed to anyone that would listen to him that those pastors were going to burn in hell.

I believe he felt more spiritual when he needed money. He felt more comfortable when he was poor and had difficulties. We lived in Southern California, but he never enjoyed the benefits of living in Orange County. He never went to the beach or to Disneyland, or even to the movies. He wouldn't allow himself to have any pleasure if there were people on the planet that were suffering. In fact, there was a season when he lived with me that he slept on the floor in the upstairs office. He wouldn't sleep on a comfortable bed if his friends in the Philippines didn't have a comfortable bed.

The term, *he was his own worst enemy* was never more true of someone. He was an electrician (but never got a license). He had the potential to easily make a couple hundred thousand a year. But he always seemed to sabotage his employment opportunities. If a job was going well, he would subconsciously sabotage it by demonstrating flakey behavior to the boss or by getting into disputes with other workers.

He had a subconscious glitch, a line of programming code that told him, "I need money." Instead of the *I need money* internal command causing him to hold onto money, the repeating subconscious belief merged into his identity. *I need money* was part of his identity. It was how he viewed himself and who he was. If he had money, he would quickly spend, give, or squander it away, so his reality lined up with what he believed about himself. Not having money was his comfort zone.

Remember, *you are who you think you are, or you become it.* Since he believed he was poor and he needed money, there was a drive in him that caused his circumstances to line up with his identity.

A *poverty mentality*, whether it causes a person to hoard money or waste money, is like a computer program that is always running in the background. It's like an app on your phone that is burning up your battery without you knowing it. It isn't something that a person thinks about, but wrong mindsets about money often sabotage a person's financial success.

Your Normal

Women that quickly bounce back to their skinny body after having a child, don't necessarily have a better metabolism than women that don't. Losing weight isn't just easier for them. Their comfort zone dives their habits. They don't feel like themselves when carrying 20, 30, or 40 extra pounds. Sure, they may put in the effort to lose weight, but the real driving force is their comfort zone. Their outward circumstances, or in this case, their body, must line up with their identity.

Our beliefs and behaviors are driven from our subconscious mind, not our conscious mind. What is resident in our subconscious mind guides, nudges, steers, and even pushes our actions or inactions. We can make all the New Year's Resolutions we want but we will fail when we get fatigued or let our guard down. Why?

Because it is our identity that needs changing. What we believe about ourselves will determine our income level, our weight, our relationship status, and our happiness.

But God

I know people who have had terrible childhoods. Some of their stories would certainly bring tears to your eyes. But today, they are not just surviving, they are thriving. Several of them are highly successful even though they grew up in poverty. For them, it was God that made the difference.

I have used this analogy in another book, but it bears repeating. Our Christian walk is like the *Wizard of Oz*. Before we *sell out* to God, our life is in black and white. We don't go to full color until we have the Holy Spirit living in us. The ruby slippers are symbolic of our faith. The witch represents the devil who is trying to steal our faith.

The Yellow Brick Road is our journey in life. Along our journey, we will encounter the Scarecrow, the Tin man, and the Lion. The Scarecrow wanted a brain. In our journey, we will have the opportunity to develop the mind of Christ. God will teach us godly wisdom as we grow in spiritual maturity. The Tin man wanted a heart. In our walk with God, the Holy Spirit will help us understand the love of God. We will love others, and we will understand God's love for us. And finally, the

Cowardly Lion wanted courage. In our spiritual journey, we develop boldness. As we mature, we should acquire fearlessness when it comes to evil. In our experiences, we have fought demons and won. We understand the authority of the believer and we know, in our gut, that God with us is greater than any demon, storm, or challenge we may face.

Our identity changes the more we develop our relationship with God. Our mind, heart, and boldness are greater and stronger even if it means that our old comfort zones have to take a back seat.

Our Capacity

Proverbs 4:20-23 says, *(20) "My son, give attention to my words; incline your ear to my sayings, (21) Do not let them depart from your eyes; Keep them in the midst of your heart; (22) For they are life to those who find them, and health to all their flesh. (23) Keep your heart with all diligence, for out of it springs the issues of life."*

The word *issues* in verse 23 can also be translated as *boundaries*. This passage tells us to pay attention to the word of God. Meditate on the word. Rehearse the written word (logos) and the spoken word (rhema) that God has spoken over you. God's word can literally change our internal boundaries. Keep your heart with all diligence, for out of it springs the boundaries of life. Our comfort zones and subconscious limitations we set on ourselves can be stretched when we allow God to do a work in our heart.

Isaiah 54:2 says, *"Enlarge the place of your tent, and let them stretch out the curtains of your dwellings; do not spare; lengthen your cords and strengthen your stakes."* God will expand our territory. He will broaden our comfort zones.

How does He do it? God speaks hope to us before the blessing is a reality. The verse right before *"the enlarge your tent'* verse says, *"Sing, O baron, you who have not borne, Break forth with singing, and cry aloud. You who have not labored with child; for more are the children of the desolate, than the children of the married woman, says the Lord."* (Isaiah 54:1)

It is not uncommon for God to give us impossible dreams. A baron woman is a woman who can't have children. Yet, God is speaking over her that she will have more children than a woman who is not baron.

God expands our capacity and our comfort levels, before He brings the blessings into our lives. He gives us destiny promises that grow within us. God may give us dreams of having enough money to bless the homeless. God may show us a vision of preaching to thousands of people. The Holy Spirit may highlight a verse that talks about marriage to prepare us for marriage. Even if certain things are beyond our comfort zone, the Holy Spirit can give us a desire for it when we know it is an assignment from God and tied to our purpose.

Sometimes, our comfort zones, *diseases of the soul*, and wrong subconscious glitches can stifle the life changing words/promises that God speaks over us. Most people don't want to let go of fear, comfort, and carnality, so we can consciously or subconsciously reject the identity-shaping words that the Holy Spirit is trying to engrain in us.

Let's do an exercise. Ask yourself some questions and journal the answers.

Money

- What is the highest income you have made in one year?
- What happened to that job? Could you have done something to sabotage it?
- What income range is within your comfort zone?
- How long have you been inside that range?
- What reasons or excuses have you allowed that limits your career?
- Is added education or certifications needed in order to excel?
- Are you happy in your current job?
- Are you afraid of added responsibility or added work?

Ask God to open your eyes and make you aware if your comfort zones have limited your success. Ask Him some "yes" or "no" questions and be open to what He tells you. Repent, if it is needed and ask God to show you the path He has for you.

Weight

· Is there a weight range that you typically gravitate to?

Ask God to tell you the weight He wants you to be. Ask Him to give you mental pictures of yourself as healthy and fit. Ask Him to give you memorable dreams of you at your desired weight. Dreams are a product of our subconscious, so we need to get a new view of ourselves in our subconscious mind. If we change our identity, our outward reality will follow.

Relationships

· If you are single and would like a relationship, are you sabotaging the possibilities by not allowing yourself to step out of your comfort zone?

Millions of people fall into this category. They limit how God can bring a person into their lives. They refuse to join a Christian dating app. They won't go to any Christian *single mingle* events in their city. They tell God how they want it to happen and when it doesn't happen how and when they want, they blame God. There is nothing wrong with stepping outside of your comfort zone, trying different things. The worst thing that can happen is you would meet some new people.

Conclusion

Most people are not aware that they have subconscious limitations and boundaries. But being aware of their existence and evaluating yourself is the first step in expanding your borders. You don't have to live by an invisible limitation that is self-imposed. God wants more for you. He wants you to succeed in every realm of life. Please, do a little self-reflection and make yourself step out in boldness to do things that are uncomfortable.

Chapter 5

The Blame-Shifting Ditch

A lot of drama in our life is caused by how we process events in our life. I am sure if we were to think about it, we have all witnessed friends or family members not taking responsibility for their own actions and blaming others for the problems they face. Misdiagnosing blame can be dangerous and can lead to a life of self-delusion if steps are not taken to correct it.

It is important to correct that behavior pattern early, so it doesn't become infused into a person. The longer the habit of blame-shifting lasts, the more engrained it can become in a person and the more delusional they can become.

When a friend's daughter was in elementary school, there were times when she forgot her backpack and then blamed her mother. Her mother packed her lunch, gather all her homework, and put everything in her backpack. She set it by the door for her daughter to grab on the way out. The daughter knew it was her responsibility to grab it. However, she shifted the blame to her mother if she got to the car and didn't have it in her hands.

Blame-shifting is a bad habit that affects people of all ages. A friend of mine, that is 20 years older than me, got mad at me a few times when she forgot something. Rather than her acknowledging that she forgot it, she pinned the blame on me because I failed to remind her. Granted, her memory isn't what it used to be. But that doesn't mean that it's okay for her to make me the scapegoat. I called her out on her blame-shifting. Not because I don't want to take the blame, but because I wanted her to recognize that habit. She has blame-shifted in other scenarios as well. It wasn't just memory issues. There have been a couple of occasions when something broke or she made a mistake. Rather than taking responsibility for her part of the mishap, she shifted the blame to someone else and labeled them as the main problem.

Years ago, I started to get frustrated with a roommate because when I went to take a jar of garlic out of the refrigerator, it fell, and half of the garlic spilled out. My roommate didn't screw the lid on the jar. Because there were several other items around the jar, I picked it up by the lid. Sure, I could have blamed her for not screwing on the lid. It was a bad habit of hers not to put lids and caps on things. However, I corrected myself because I was the one who tried to pick up the jar by the lid instead of moving the other items out of the way and grabbing the jar around the middle.

This example oversimplifies what we do so often. There is something in human nature that wants to point the finger of blame at someone or something else. We overlook the role we played in the situation and point the fault at others.

Here is another example. A while back a roommate of mine got very angry with me and blamed me when she caught a cold. There were germs in the house because my daughter had a cold. My daughter mostly stayed in her room but her germs were probably in the upstairs bathroom that they shared. I had warned my roommate that there were germs in the house and told her she needed to protect her immunity. Yet, that week she had started dating a new guy. On the nights she wasn't out late with him, she was on the phone with him until the wee hours of the morning. She wasn't getting enough sleep, staying warm, eating right, or being germ-conscious. But in her mind, it was all my fault that she caught a cold.

Again, human nature wants us to blame someone or something for a negative situation instead of taking personal responsibility for our role in unfortunate circumstances. Most negative situations have multiple contributing factors and if we are focused on just one aspect of it, we are missing the whole picture.

There is a difference between occasional blame-shifting and having a *victim mentality*. They have the same root, but a person with a *victim mentality* can't see the error of their ways. That wrong mindset has embedded itself into the person's identity. And they truly believe they are not to blame for situations and circumstances in their life. The difference is self-awareness. The person that occasionally blame-shifts can self-correct, or they will be open-minded if someone brings the blame-shifting to their attention.

The Victim Mentality

There are some common traits of those who have a *victim mentality*. The obvious trait is they identify others as the cause for undesired situations.

- "The lady in front of me in line made me late."
- "I didn't finish the project because the teacher wasn't clear about the assignment."
- "The vase broke because there was something oily on it. It wasn't my fault it slipped out of my hand."
- "It's not my fault my car got impounded. My job doesn't pay me enough for me to pay my car registration."

In each of these situations, the person could have taken actions so the issue wouldn't have happened. In the first scenario, it wasn't the lady in front of him that made him late. They either left the house late and didn't give themselves enough time to run the errands. With the second excuse, the student could have approached the teacher after class to get clarity on the assignment if they didn't understand it. With the third mishap, if a person was carrying a vase that felt oily, they could have put it down to wipe off the oil or they could have supported the vase from the bottom with their other hand. And lastly, it takes six months of having an expired registration before the highway patrol would have the car impounded. In those six months, and certainly before it expired, the person could have saved money or done something to earn more money to meet that financial obligation.

Another common trait in those with a *victim mentality* is they will oftentimes be hypervigilant around others. According to www.healthline.com, "Hypervigilance is a state of heightened alertness and sensitivity to potential threats, often resulting from trauma or stress. It involves the nervous system inaccurately filtering sensory information, leading individuals to constantly access their surroundings for danger, whether real or perceived. This condition can manifest through symptoms such as anxiety, irritability, and difficulty concentrating, and is commonly associated with PTSD."

Hypervigilance is really being in *fight or flight* mode all the time. A person wears a negative filter where they expect to be harmed by others. And when someone has that perspective, they can turn innocent interactions with others into dramatic situations. Drama follows them because they expect it.

Another common trait of a person with a *victim mentality* is they assume others have negative intentions. They are highly suspicious of most everyone, and they will choose to see the worst in people. Even if someone is doing something kind for them, they will assume that person has ulterior motives.

Another common mindset that people with a *victim mentality* have is that they believe most people are just more fortunate than them. They see the success that others around them have, and they believe that other people have more talent, skills, money, or luck than they have. Many people incorrectly believe that God graced other people with more in life than they got. They think they drew the short straw. They fail to recognize that it is the choices we make in life that cause our success. Most people have complicated challenges in their life. It is what they do that makes the difference in whether or not they overcome and thrive. Most success has to do with a person's belief structure, how they process information, and their internal fortitude. Very little of their status in life has to do with how smart they are or their natural abilities.

Most people with a *victim mentality* crave empathy. When others sympathize with their struggles, it makes them feel validated and it reinforces their wounded outlook. Many of these people will share their woes with anyone who will listen. Their problems are their excuses. They will often feel offended if a person dismisses or minimizes their trials and tribulations. Don't dare show them a silver lining or discuss ways to get out of their pit. If you do, they will most likely brand you as a cold-hearted soul who just doesn't understand their life.

People with a *victim mentality* are usually introspective and defensive. They tend to divide people into good or bad with no gray zone between them. They are unadventurous. They are generally unwilling to take even small and calculated risks. If an opportunity is presented to them, they will usually exaggerate the likelihood of a negative outcome. They also exhibit a learned helplessness. They underestimate their ability or influence, often feeling powerless. This helpless mindset helps them justify to themselves and others why they can't make changes to improve their lives. And finally, they are usually self-abasing and will put themselves down.

A person that has a *victim mentality* usually won't admit that they have it, either to themselves or others. They don't see it.

My brother Ken, who I mentioned in the last chapter, had a *victim mentality*. Every problem in his life was someone else's fault. His money problems weren't his wrong mindsets or the fact that he sent all his money to women in the Philippines. His problems were because of his boss or a demanding customer, and even ultimately our father.

My brother Ken believed the reason he wasn't successful in life was because our father kicked him out of the house at 27 years old. He blame-shifted all his financial problems onto our father because he had to get a job and support himself at 27 years old.

Ken was a year and a half older than me. I moved out at 19 years old, but Ken was the last of the seven children to live at home with our parents. Our father told Ken he could live at home, rent free, as long as he was going to college. Ken could have finished college by the age of 22. However, my brother dropped out of every class he registered for at the local junior college. He registered for classes, but dropped them, semester after semester, year after year. In that ten-year period between his graduation from high school and him turning 27 years old, I don't think he finished any classes. But in Ken's mind, he couldn't finish college and make something of his life because he got asked to leave home when he was 27.

Ken was a very skilled electrician, but he refused to complete the certification process. He procrastinated and didn't have the discipline to take the courses. He purchased the courses a couple of times but never did them. He didn't even need the full college degree to be successful. He could have just completed the on-line electrician courses and could have had a very successful and prosperous life. There was nothing wrong with his cognitive ability. He was smart. He just chose to procrastinate everything.

Ken didn't just blame-shift. He embodied the other *victim mentality* traits as well. He was hypervigilant. He assumed the worst about everyone. He had an ability to make everyone evil in his mind. He acted helpless in situations and put himself down. He wasn't adventurous. He wouldn't allow himself to do anything that could be considered fun. He checked all the boxes. I will add a box. Ken also re-wrote history, and he added false details that strengthened his perspective of the past that just weren't true.

The Homeless

I have a heart of compassion for homeless people and those facing homelessness. I carry an assignment from God to help them. That help not only means helping them with shelter, it also means helping them emotionally and spiritually.

It has been my observation that a high percentage of homeless people and people that are about to become homeless have a *victim mentality*. Several of the ones I have spoken to do have many of the common traits of a *victim mentality* that I mentioned in the section above.

Back in the late 90's, a woman who heard that I was helping people wrote me a letter that was several pages long about her life and her situation. She was homeless and was reaching out for help. She felt the need to share all of her troubles with me and told me about everyone that has mistreated her and those that didn't help her. I'm sure as the lady was writing it, she didn't see anything wrong with her perspective. But almost every sentence oozed *victim mentality*. She didn't take any personal responsibility for her situation. Everyone did her wrong.

It is my belief that some homeless people unknow-ingly guided themselves into a *victim mentality*. Let me explain. Like many people, they had a habit of blame-shifting. When their living situation started to turn dire, they froze like a *deer in the headlights*. They didn't know how to handle it, so they reverted their thinking to a helpless mindset. When they would talk to people about their situation, they gave all the external reasons and omitted the actions or inactions on their part that contributed to the problem. They had to tell their story about how they became homeless so many times that they started to believe the version they told people. As a result, it further engrained the reality they were choosing to embrace.

Simple blame-shifting is a ditch. But a *victim mentality* is a deeper pit that many people can't get out of themselves because they can't see how their beliefs are delusional. Someone who has a *victim mentality* does have a mental disability. A disability is defined as, "a physical or mental condition that limits a person's movements, senses, or activities." Well, a *victim mentality* does limit a person's ability to help themselves. They often convince themselves that they can't work. They set unrealistic expectations of others. They refuse to take specific steps that would help themselves and they won't allow themselves to view situations from other people's perspectives.

I recently had a conversation with a woman who had been homeless but was now living with someone. She wasn't completely delusional in her *victim mentality*, but she could head in that direction if she didn't change some of her views on situations. To use the ditch analogy, she was in a 3-foot ditch, not an 8-foot pit. If she corrected some of her wrong attitudes, it would absolutely be possible for her to break her wrong mindsets.

She was 38 years old, and she blamed her parents for being homeless because they kicked her out of the house. In my first three conversations with her, she has mentioned that each time. Most of the conversations I had with her were spiritual and we discussed demonic activity. She talked about how often she saw demons. She even said that was the reason her parents kicked her out of the house, because she saw demonic entities. I am the author of *Real Stories of Angels, Demons, and the Supernatural* so we mostly chatted about the spiritual world. However, by the third conversation, I realized she was metaphorically *dipping her toes* into the pool of a *victim mentality* mindset.

She receives $1,000 a month from the government as a mental health disability. She said she doesn't want to get a job because two people making minimum wage can't afford to rent in Orange County, California. At the time of this writing, minimum wage is $15 an hour, and if someone worked full time, they would make $2,600 a month. If she and her roommate worked full time at minimum wage that would be $5,200 a month. Cheap rent here in Orange County would be $2,800 a month. So, it's doable but not comfortable. Besides a single person could always rent a room for $800 to $1,200 a month if they found a landlord that would take them. However, that would be a challenge since most landlords want someone who makes more money.

They want excellent credit, income, references, and a job history before they would be considered. So, renting in Orange County, California is difficult.

I tried to encourage her to look for work that paid more than the minimum wage. She said she really wants to renovate houses, fix them up, and re-sell them. That would be her dream job.

I said the best thing to do would be to work for a company that does that so she would learn the business. She immediately said she won't work for someone else. She would only do it if she was her own boss.

I am a real estate broker, so I have knowledge of the industry. I asked her how she was going to get the skill to renovate homes if she wasn't willing to work for someone else. She didn't have an answer to that question. I also told her that that buyers these days require that renovations be made by licensed contractors, and many buyers require permits for those remodels as a condition of the purchase.

I asked her, "if someone sponsored you and paid for you to go to a trade school to learn construction and renovations, would you go?" She said, "no" and that was the end of that texting session.

She was not willing to work minimum wage jobs. She was not willing to receive formal training in the field of work she desires. She was not willing to be an employee for someone else.

She basically said her employment was going to be on her terms and she wasn't willing to see the flaws in her logic.

She had a bad experience when she had a telemarketing job and that made her believe all jobs were like that. Telemarketing is a terrible job where you face constant rejection and unrealistic sales goals. But there are good jobs out there that a person can actually enjoy and find fulfillment in. But in her mind, she labeled and categorized working as an employee as bad.

From my observation, she had a sense of entitlement, like the world has to conform to meet her self-dictated rules. I would like to help her, but she would need to see her wrong mindset and want to change.

There is no fast track for career success. Before I started my own real estate brokerage, I had to hang my real estate salesperson's license under a well-established real estate company, so I received the experience I needed. I also had to study, take quizzes, and take a state exam in order to receive my real estate broker's license. I had to save up, plan, and conquer my own fears before I started my own company. Success is a series of steps. Typically, a person doesn't go from A to Z overnight. They need the steps in-between to learn and develop their skills.

Whether a person is homeless or is about to be homeless, they should take an inventory of their belief system. Are they going to be a *deer in the headlights* and let negative stuff just happen to them? Are they going to agree with fear and negative self-talk that tells them that they can't make it? Are they going to say "no" to the steps that would get them out of the pit just because they are uncomfortable?

Reset

If you find that you tend to blame-shift or you have even adopted some *victim mentality* behavior patterns, there are things you can do to correct it. If you are hypervigilant, going on walks can actually help. Studies have shown that simply walking mimics your heart rate of when you were in the womb. Your brain subconsciously connects that to feelings of comfort and safety.

Another thing you can do is to pay attention to what you allow yourself to hear. Don't watch violent and suspense-filled videos and movies. If you listen to music, only listen to uplifting and encouraging music. Don't feed fear and anxiety. Recognize when you are in a *fight or flight* state and do things to reverse that.

Pay attention to the thoughts that you accept as truth. Do 2 Corinthians 10:5 and take your thoughts captive. Pay attention to them. Instead of rehearsing why another person is to blame, examine the situation from different angles. Journal the things that you may have done that contributed to the situation. Recognize that most situations are not black and white. There usually isn't one victim and one villain. Most of the time, there are multiple shades of gray with the people involved. Negative situations usually have several contributing factors that have caused specific outcomes. Allow yourself to see those even if it means acknowledging that you were to blame or partially to blame for the incident. Were you unwilling to compromise? Did your fear cause you to not step out of your comfort zone? What other mindsets influenced the circumstance?

Next, ask God to lead and guide you. Regardless of past mistakes, your past doesn't dictate your future. You can turn your situation around. Lean into God. Be willing to repent and change. And watch God lead you into a better season.

Chapter 6

The Depression Ditch

According to Google, 13% of the U.S. population is on anti-depressants. I'm not surprised. Every time I have a doctor's appointment, whether it be face-to-face, or a telephone appointment, the nurse always asks me if I am experiencing depression. The medical industry is very quick to prescribe pharmaceuticals to treat emotional symptoms. I am not against anti-depressants. I merely want to point out the sheer numbers of people that feel their depression is so bad that they need medical intervention for it.

Another statistic shows that nearly 60 million Americans (one in four) suffer from mental illness which includes clinical depression, bi-polar disorder, schizophrenia, or OCD. According to Forbes, approximately 21 million Americans have experienced a major depression episode. A recent Gallop poll showed that 29% of Americans have been diagnosed with depression during their lifetime. And that 29% may be low because that is the percentage of people that reported it. I'm sure there are millions more that were hesitant to report it. So, the numbers are quite large.

This chapter will discuss depression from several different angles, including spiritual, psychological, and medical causes. But first, I want to highlight how depression can be a ditch.

When a person is disheartened, disappointed, discouraged, and wallowing in despair, they won't take action to improve their life. They will sit in that pit and not even try to claw their way out. Depression can not only delay success, but it can also sabotage and derail someone's life all together. A person can lose their job, their relationships, and their money if they allow themselves to drown in the cauldron of their depression.

The level of depression they are in will determine their willingness and strength to even try to fight it.

That is why it is so critical to address it and fight it while it is still only discouragement or disappointment, because once it reaches full-fledged depression, it may be much harder to fight. Depression is typically progressive and there are beginning stages of it that can be easier to fix than some of the later stages of depression.

When I was doing research for my book. *The Suicide Snare*, I read that depression was caused by the lack of hope. A person entrenched in depression embraces the thought that their situation isn't going to change. If someone tries to offer them hope, they will typically reject it and not believe it. That is why it is vitally important to speak hopeful words to those close to you that may be struggling with discouragement or depression.

The Mayo Clinic website says that depression is caused by genetics, brain chemicals, or a person's life situation. While those things are factors, I believe there are more contributing factors than just these. I believe the spirit world plays a significant role in depression. I believe a person's personality temperament and soul iniquities are also factors in whether a person has a bent towards depression.

Spiritual Attacks

This may be brand new information for some people, but the spirit world is around us all the time. There are angels and demons present in most environments we enter. I also believe Christians have a guardian angel and they probably have a demon or two assigned to them.

The spirit world is empowered by our agreement. We can activate angels to work on our behalf by quoting Bible verses. Psalms 103:20 says, *"Bless the Lord, you His angels, who excel in strength, who do His word, heeding the voice of His word."* What we say is very important. Proverbs 18:21 says, *"Death and life are in the power of the tongue, and those who love it will eat its fruit."* We can speak life, God's word, over situations and that gets the attention of angels to fulfill God's word. Angels do His word! Angels heed the verbalization of His word.

That old adage from the 16th century of an angel sitting on one shoulder and a demon sitting on the other is truer than people realize. Demons will whisper suggestions to us all the time. The demon assigned to you will masquerade as your own thoughts and will masquerade as the voice of the Holy Spirit. Where the adage is wrong is, the angel won't whisper in your ear. Rather the Holy Spirit within you will speak to you if you are spiritually sensitive and know how to register His voice. However, the demon assigned to you will mimic your own thoughts to the point where you believe those thoughts are your own.

While this chapter discusses different aspects that influence whether a person has a propensity towards depression, it's important to acknowledge that depression is a spirit. Isaiah 61:3 says, *"To console those who mourn in Zion; to give them beauty for ashes, the oil of joy for mourning, the garment of praise for the spirit of heaviness."* The last part of that verse labels heaviness as a spirit. That metaphorical dark cloud over a person isn't just their negative circumstances, personality, brain chemicals, or psychological wounds. There is a spiritual component when a person is depressed.

A month or so before writing this chapter, there was a three-day period where I kept hearing, "I'm depressed." I typically don't get depressed, and I will discuss that more in the personality section of this book. But I kept hearing "I'm depressed." I understood at the time that a demon was trying to impersonate my own thoughts. It was trying to get me to agree with the suggestion. I thought it was strange that it was trying to do a spiritual attack on me because there were a couple situations in my life that had improved. Sure, lots of areas in my life were not ideal, but my circumstances were not terrible.

In retrospect, I now think that demonic suggestion wasn't necessarily from a regular demon that has been assigned to me. A couple of weeks before then a new tenant had moved into a rental unit that is attached to the main house where I am living. I think that demon that harassed me for a few days was one that was assigned to the new tenant. And today, two weeks to the day of my writing this chapter, that tenant committed suicide.

On a Saturday night, two weeks ago, between 9:30 pm and 1:30 am, I heard him bumping around the tenant area of the house. There is a deadbolt lock that separates the tenant area and the main part of the house. The tenants have their own entrances, bathrooms, refrigerators, and kitchen. The tenants never come into the main section of the house. That night I heard him walking hard. There weren't any voices, no crying, no knocking, banging, or other attempts to get anyone's attention. I heard loud walking and even some stumbling. At first, I assumed he was sick or drunk. But I didn't hear the toilet flush or vomiting, so I ruled out sickness. I couldn't understand why he went back and forth from his bedroom to the bathroom so many times. If he needed something, I assumed he would call to me, or knock on that hallway door, or at least bang on a wall or door to get my attention.

The next afternoon, I noticed that his car hadn't moved, and I didn't hear him moving around so I texted him. After a while with no response, I entered through the dead bolted hallway. I discovered a bloody bathroom, and his bedroom door was open. I peeked my head in and saw him on the floor. He had slit his own throat.

Let me be clear. I believe homicide, suicide, and self-harm are always driven by demonic suggestions. John 10:10 says, *"The thief does not come except to steal, and to kill, and to destroy. I have come that they may have life, and that they may have it more abundantly."* That is the goal for the kingdom of darkness. They want to kill, steal, and destroy. And the easiest way to do it is to get a person to do it to themselves. We need to recognize depression and suicidal thoughts for what they are. They aren't just a person feeling sad. They are a spiritual attack on a person's life.

One of the names of Satan in the Bible is Beelzebub (Matt. 12:24) which is translated as the *Lord of the Flies*. Think about that for a moment. That is one of the ways the devil attacks people. The mental attacks are like flies swarming around your head trying to land with negative thoughts. You swat one away, and then another tries to land on you. Demonic whispers will try to masquerade as your own thoughts and convince you that your situation is hopeless and that you should end your life.

This is discussed more in my book, *The Suicide Snare*. In that book, I share the story of the boyfriend I had that killed himself. I discussed the demons he encountered as well as some other suicide demon stories.

I didn't know the tenant that killed himself very well. He had only lived in that room for one month. He was 31 years old, tall, handsome, muscular, had excellent credit, and a high paying job. He had everything going for him. Yet, a demon convinced him that he should end his life. He was sad over the breakup of a girlfriend, but he seemed okay in the few encounters I had with him. I did encourage him to seek God in a text a couple weeks earlier. I didn't know his religious background, but I mentioned in my text to him that I was in Christian ministry. He knew he could talk to me if he was struggling but he chose not to. One thing I want to mention is, the last noise I heard was around 1:30 am on Sunday morning. I knew it was 1:30 because I heard the Holy Spirit say, "He's at peace." At the time, I assumed that meant he was going to bed, and he would finally sleep it off. But a few days later, the choice of words dawned on me. The Holy Spirit wouldn't tell me, "He's at peace" if he went to hell. There is nothing peaceful about hell. The Holy Spirit could have said, "It's over." I believe he either had an existing relationship with God, or he made peace with God while he was waiting to pass. I also think I registered the time it started and when it stopped because I was supposed to communicate that information to the coroner and sheriff when they were doing their investigation.

I wish people had more understanding of the spirit realm. I wish they learned how to *take every thought captive,* as it says in 2 Cor. 10:5. I wish they wouldn't allow random, unfettered, negative thoughts to assail their minds.

There are a couple of additional details I want to mention. This suicide wasn't something that he had planned for a long time. Again, I didn't know him, so I didn't know if he was prone to depression or suicidal thoughts. However, I am the one who cleaned his blood from the bathroom and the bedroom, and I am the one who cleaned out his refrigerator. The refrigerator was full of food he had just bought. He had more than 10 lbs. of expensive beef in his refrigerator drawer. He had two full cartons of eggs. He had lots of fruit and vegetables. If he had been planning this for a while, he wouldn't have just bought so much food.

Additionally, when I was cleaning the blood smudges in his room, I discovered a little baggie of drugs. There was a one-inch by two-inch plastic bag with white powder in it on a white dresser that was in his closet. The homicide detectives must have missed it when they were here because the powder and the dresser were the same color.

After I discovered the drugs, it suddenly made sense to me why I kept hearing him walk from his bedroom to the bathroom so many times that night. He was high on something.

I understand the desire for people that are depressed to turn to alcohol or drugs to numb the pain and even silence the noise in their head. But drugs and alcohol just make it worse! When a person is under the influence, they are far more likely to agree with demonic whispers and suggestions. Most people cooperate with demonic suggestions and commands when they are drunk or high. Their defenses are down, and they lack their normal reasoning abilities.

There are absolutely medical and psychological factors that influence a person's propensity for depression. But we cannot ignore the spiritual side to it. The enemy is out to *kill, steal, and destroy* and he will try to take you out by your own hand.

Educate yourself on spiritual entities and understand your spiritual authority. Learn to pay attention to your thoughts and recognize their origin. Understand that you have been targeted by the kingdom of darkness because you have the potential to be an enormous threat.

Personality Temperaments

Since this is intended to be a mini book, I'm not going to do an in-depth teaching on personality types. But I will mention that the four basic types: sanguine, choleric, melancholic, and phlegmatic, have been around for thousands of years.

Carl Jung researched and expanded the area of personality types. Later, a mother daughter team (Myers and Briggs) developed a personality indictor questionnaire, the MBTI during World War II. Then later, in the 80's and 90's, Keirsey and Bates, built on the Myers Briggs 16 personality type model. They expanded the teaching to include how each type functioned as a child, parent, student, employee, etc.

When it comes to depression, there are certain personality types that have a stronger pull towards depression than other types. In the four major type model, the melancholy and even phlegmatic types have greater propensity for depression. Melancholy people tend to get their feelings hurt more often and they can carry grudges. They can have anxiety where they rehearse negative thoughts over and over again in their mind. And they feel emotional pain and passion in a stronger way than some of the other types. Phlegmatic types can also lean into depression since they often internalize and overthink situations. For the most part, choleric types may be too action oriented in trying to fix the problems to allow themselves to sink too low into depression. And the Sanguine types are usually more optimistic than the other types and their thinking tends to lean more on the positive side.

I do think the more comprehensive 16 personality type study is fascinating. I am an ESFP. And as an ESFP, I tend to look for the silver lining in situations. ESFPs are optimists. We usually don't have strongholds of fear, and we don't typically have anxiety. Certainly, we can get discouraged and disappointed, but we are not hardwired with a propensity for depression.

That is why hearing "I'm depressed" for three days surprised me. That isn't how I am hardwired, and I don't recall ever hearing that before. I understood it was demonic whispers because those aren't thoughts that I naturally think.

Soul Iniquities

Soul iniquities or *diseases of the soul* are subconscious propensities towards certain types of sin. I briefly mentioned them in Chapter One. They are taught in my books, *Diseases of the Soul*, and *Blind Spots and Wrinkles*.

As a reminder, diseases of the soul are like cancer inside our soul. Just like there are different types of cancer, there are different types of soul iniquities. Like cancer, they can go undetected for years before their damage is discovered. They can grow and metastasize without us even knowing that they are silently killing aspects of our life. They can subtly influence our beliefs and behaviors and can sabotage our relationships, finances, careers, and destinies.

They are: 1) pride, 2) fear, 3) unforgiveness/offense, 4) jealousy/envy, 5) rebellion, 6) religious pride, 7) prejudice/hatred, 8) weak willpower/lack of discipline, 9) sexual sins, addictions, and fetishes, 10) idolatry, 11) greed/selfish ambition, and 12) negative, critical, or judgmental mindset.

Soul iniquities are not the root cause of depression, but they can greatly influence it. Pride leads to deceptive thinking. So, if a person has a lot of pride in their subconscious mind they can believe all kinds of false narratives. Pride will cause a person to only believe their version of truth so it will make it difficult for them to change their perspective. Someone with a stronghold of fear will most likely have anxiety. They will rehearse negative, fearful thoughts over and over in their mind, which can cause them to sink deeper and deeper into depression. Someone with a root of unforgiveness/offense can get so emotionally hurt that they will dwell on that emotional trauma to the point of not allowing themselves to see a different viewpoint of the situation. A person with a lack of discipline won't force themselves to get out of bed. Even though they know that getting outside or taking a shower will help their mental state, many of those that lack discipline will allow themselves to stay in bed. And finally, someone who has a stronghold of a critical spirit, will usually just focus on the negative aspects of life. They will rehearse negative details about themselves and others and won't allow themselves to see the positive attributes. Rehearsing negative views over and over will cause a person to spiral into deeper levels of despair.

Brain Chemicals

There are four primary brain chemicals that produce positive emotions. They are dopamine, oxytocin, serotonin, and endorphins (sometimes referred to as D.O.S.E.). These happy brain chemicals affect our emotions, mood, energy level, learning capacity, sex drive, and sleeping patterns.

Psychiatrists prescribe anti-depressants to try to re-balance the brain chemicals. When a person is depressed, their brain isn't producing these happy brain chemicals like it should. Medications may be helpful, but they are not the solution. Our brain chemistry follows our thoughts. If we rehearse negative thoughts all day, it changes our brain chemistry and depletes our happy brain chemicals. What we think about all day can change our D.O.S.E. chemicals.

A problem with taking anti-depressants is, it can influence our identity. If we wake up in the morning and we rehearse in our mind, "I am a depressed person," we allow that thought to become part of our identity. If we identify as a depressed person, it will make it more difficult to change. Our identity, what we believe about ourselves, dictates our success in life. A person that struggles with depression or anxiety needs to guard against branding themselves as permanently depressed or anxious in their subconscious mind. They may be going through a season, but that season shouldn't permanently change their self-identity.

Life Situations

Certainly, life circumstances can nudge a person towards depression. Some people go through extremely difficult things that cause them to lose hope and even lose the will to live. Traumatic events can happen when there is a loss of a loved one, a career, wealth, or reputation. There can be others who may have made mistakes, and they are riddled with guilt. The mental torment of their failures and weaknesses drives them to depression.

Recently, a doctor friend of mine called me crying. She said she didn't want to live anymore. She has had a terrible last two years. Her boyfriend broke up right after her twin sister passed away. The boyfriend said he wanted someone who was younger. They argued and he filed a restraining order against her. He said he feared for his life. He is a six-foot tall man and weighs approximately two hundred pounds. She is approximately five feet tall and weighs about 110 lbs. He said he was afraid of her. He told the court that he couldn't sleep and was traumatized. Yet, the same day he made those claims to the court, he posted pictures on his social media with his new girlfriend saying he has never been happier.

One night, the ex-boyfriend got my friend arrested for violating the restraining order because she was too close to where his boat was docked. She wasn't in his dock but she was in the harbor area. She was in her car and even moved the car a few spaces to be further away. However, since she had had a couple of glasses of wine that night, she got a DUI. She wasn't over the alcohol limit with the breathalyzer, but because she was emotionally upset, the police officer said she failed the field sobriety test. She wasn't drunk and she wasn't driving but she ended up in jail and received a D.U.I.

The ex-boyfriend ruined her life. He filed a complaint with the medical board referencing the restraining order, the arrest, and the D.U.I. My friend had been a doctor for more than 30 years but ended up losing her medical license. Between the legal fees and medical board fees, she didn't have the money to fight it. She was forced to surrender her license for a minimum of three years.

Needless to say, my friend was devastated. She was broke, jobless, and emotionally crushed. When she talked to me, she went from sadness, to despair, then to anger. By the end of the conversation, she was yelling in anger.

In the few times that we spoke, she kept repeating the same thing. I told her to stop repeating the emotional wounds. I told her it leads to a cycle of sadness, despair, then anger and it's emotionally exhausting. It's not sustainable. She started drinking too much and too often as a way of escape, but it only made it worse. The more she drank, the more despair and anger roared within her. The mental stress of it was taking too much of a toll. I told her to focus on positive, uplifting things.

She asked, "what is positive and uplifting?"

I said, "Watch or listen to Christian music on Youtube. Watch a comedy on TV. Watch preaching videos that revitalize your hope. By the constant negative emotion, you are affecting your brain chemicals and preventing the release of the good brain chemicals. Rehearsing the negative will drive you further and further into discouragement and depression. You are the captain of your soul! You get to decide if you are going to have a happy life. It isn't what your circumstances are. It's what you decide and will it to be. You may have lots of unanswered questions but you can set the trajectory for your life for happiness and blessings. You are what you think you are, or you become it. That's another way of saying, "as a man thinks in his heart, so is he."

That next Sunday, I saw her in church, and she came forward for prayer. She said my *pep talk* really helped her and she was doing much better.

Regardless of the losses in your life and regardless of the bumps and bruises you have sustained, your perspective changes your future. You can recover from anything if you choose the correct trajectory for your life. You set the direction for success. It's not your past, your failures, or your losses. It's what you choose it to be.

The Solution

I don't think there is a *one size fits* all type solution when it comes to depression. When a person has something wrong in their body, do you treat the symptoms or the root cause? The answer is both. Likewise, I believe understanding the root causes individually in a person is the key to helping them get out of the ditch of depression.

- What is your personality type?
- Do you have a natural propensity for discouragement and depression?
- What soul iniquities do you have?

- Is there a stronghold of fear or a negative nature?
- Is there a *generational curse* of depression in your family tree?
- Are there other psychological traumas that could be affecting you?
- Are there childhood emotional wounds that remain unhealed?
- How spiritually mature are you?
- Do you understand the spirit world?
- Do you know how to take every thought captive (2 Cor. 10:5)?
- Do you know how to recognize demonic suggestions and whispers?
- How are your brain chemicals?
- Are you doing anything to increase the positive ones? (like walking barefoot on grass and sand or spending time with pets?)
- Are you listening to encouraging music?
- Are you watching comedies on TV?

Proverbs 17:22 says, *"A merry heart does good like a medicine, but a broken spirit dries the bones."* A merry heart (laughter) is like medicine. Happy brain chemicals are released when we laugh. As well, a few studies have been conducted that showed significant mental health improvement when people read the Bible at least four days a week. Depression and anxiety were exponentially reduced by reading the Bible on a regular basis.

And finally, we must take measures to infuse hope back into our hearts. Remember, the main cause of depression was that a person feels hopeless. A person experiencing hopelessness no longer believes their negative situation can improve. So, look for *the silver lining*. Allow yourself to believe again and hope again.

One study I saw said that speaking something hopeful releases dopamine in the brain. So, brain chemicals can change when we embrace hope. We need to lean into God because He will speak hope to us. He will heal our hearts and show us a better path.

God's word tells us in Jeremiah 29:11, *"For I know the thoughts that He thinks towards you says the Lord, thoughts of peace and not of evil, to give you a future and a hope."* God wants us to excel in life. He doesn't want us to embrace fear, anxiety, or hopelessness.

Chapter 7

The Surrender Ditch

I have used the *Wizard of Oz* reference in this book in an earlier chapter. As I began this chapter, I was reminded of the *Surrender Dorothy* scene in the movie. The wicked witch was trying to get Dorothy to give up. That is what the kingdom of darkness does. They try to pressure Christians to give up.

It can be so subtle, most people miss it. We know that the demon assigned to us will masquerade as our own thoughts and will try to mimic the voice of the Holy Spirit. Most of the time when a demon suggests something to us, it doesn't register on our radar. We don't know an evil entity is whispering in our ear.

Surrendered to Sin

As I have mentioned, I am the author of *Diseases of the Soul* and *Blind Spots and Wrinkles*. Both of these books help the reader identify areas of carnality that may be residing in their subconscious mind. But the raw, honest truth is – most people don't want to know their areas of sin and weakness. They don't want to recognize areas of iniquity because then they would be responsible to God to work on them. They don't want to be called out for jealousy. They don't want their fear or unforgiveness to be labeled a sin.

Most Christians know that Romans 12:2 tells us not to be conformed this world but to be transformed by the renewing of our mind. We know the verse, but we pick and choose what that means to us. We will choose to focus on the *bless me* verses and try to get those down into our spirit. But we will steer clear of correction passages in the Bible. We may even ignore the subtle promptings of the Holy Spirit until, eventually, our conscience is seared in that area.

Many people fail to understand that we are responsible for our carnality before God whether we acknowledge its existence or not. God will hold us accountable for the assignments He has given us. Just because our sin nature may have prevented us from completing our God "to do" list, doesn't mean that we are *off the hook*. Souls are tied to our obedience to God. If we fail our assignments, it may mean multitudes won't complete their life's purpose.

It is too easy to get caught up in the busyness of life to work on our character faults. After all, we are loved and forgiven, right? Of course, we are unconditionally loved. But forgiveness comes when there is repentance. We aren't going to seek repentance for our carnality that we don't acknowledge.

Whether it's a pornography addiction, or getting drunk in private, or lying, it's all carnal behavior that is ungodly. Whether it is acknowledged or not, most people have given up trying to change. They are comfortable in the world they have created for themselves, and they have convinced themselves that God overlooks their wrongdoing. Most people rationalize and reason that other people's sin is way worse than theirs, therefore, they are okay.

Why have so many people surrendered to their carnality? Because they tried to change a few times and the negative behavior kept popping up. They haven't understood that our beliefs and behaviors are driven from our subconscious mind. They haven't heard and recognized the concept of comfort zones and *diseases of the soul*. They haven't known the manifestations of their iniquities, so they haven't been about to control it. They haven't learned how to take their thoughts captive, and they have embraced demonic whispers as their own thoughts.

Most people have metaphorically just thrown up their hands to their weaknesses and they have compartmentalized them. What does compartmentalize mean? It's an emotional defense mechanism where a person separates thoughts, feelings, or memories into distinct mental boxes to manage them more effectively. It's a strategy of the psyche to avoid feelings of anxiety, especially if there is an internal conflict.

An example of this would be a man living a double life. When he is at home with the wife and kids, he doesn't allow himself to feel guilty about his mistress on the side. When he is with the mistress, he doesn't consider how his actions would affect his family at home. Keeping the two lives separate in his mind allows him to not feel conviction or guilt for his actions.

Whether it's a porn addiction, drug or alcohol addiction, gambling, or even shopping compulsion, people have areas of their life that they allow to go unfettered. They don't try to reel it in; they simply detach that area of weakness from their sense of culpability. They don't allow themselves to feel guilty because that issue is just *swept under the rug* without repentance or accountability.

A person in this cycle usually doesn't allow themselves to move forward in the assignments of God. They will make excuses and justifications. Even though they may not consciously decide to live in defeat, they don't want to move forward and strive for success in case their secrets find them out. They would rather live in obscurity than be in the driver's seat on their journey to success. They self-sabotage because their life is fractured.

Surrendered Their Promises

We understand that there are people that have surrendered to their carnality and don't even try to fight it. But there are also people who have given up on attempting to receive blessings from God.

If you were to do a web search on how many promises are in the Bible, some postings would say 3,500. Another would say 7,000, and still another would say 8,800. The exact number is irrelevant. What is important is, the Bible is full of promises that are available for believers.

Sure, some Christians are ignorant about the promises in the Bible. Their church may not teach that we can have Sozo. (A Greek word in the Bible that means to escape destruction, to be healed, to keep safe or preserved, to be kept whole.) Some Christians don't understand faith and don't know that there are promises in the Bible that we can obtain by faith.

However, there are other believers that were taught about the promises in the Bible, but they don't try to obtain them. I understand that to some extent. They probably tried a time or two and it didn't work for them.

I think the real problem is, most Christians can agree with the faith message in their head, but that belief hasn't seeped down into their hearts. Mark 11:23 says, *"For assuredly, I say to you, whoever says to this mountain, Be removed and be cast into the sea, and does not doubt in his heart, but believes that those things he says will be done, he will have whatever he says."*

Christians can say what they want to believe all day long, but if they doubt in their heart, it isn't true faith and that mountain won't move. They assume what they believe in their head is what they believe in their heart, and that just isn't the case. The challenge becomes getting what we believe in our head to sink down into the soil of our heart.

Somewhere in most people's subconscious mind, they believe that if God truly wanted them healed, then He would zap them healed. We can hear dozens of sermons about receiving healing by faith, but we have to change that belief in our subconscious mind that says the healing has to come sovereignly.

Even if people don't work their faith for healing, the Bible is full of other promises that get ignored. They will stew for hours in fear, worry, and anxiety instead of developing their faith for peace for their minds. They will allow drama and strife to rule their household instead of standing in faith and authority to calm the atmosphere in their house.

We don't have to be victims of the devil's schemes. We can take authority in our household by binding the devil and spirits of strife and division. We can also activate angels when she speak Bible verses over our homes and family.

Surrendered Their Purpose

I attended two Bible schools in the 90's. I noticed that most Bible college students were full of zeal to obey the will of God and carry out their God assignments. Some of them are pastors today. But most of them live regular lives.

It is so easy to get caught up in the cares of this world. Afterall, to survive, we have to make money. To make money, we probably have to work long hours. It is so easy to pour our blood, sweat, and tears into a company that really doesn't care about us. We can spend all of our energy and focus on work, and we can forget our dreams and ambitions. We can not only neglect our family and friends, but we can also neglect our God assignments.

The reason some people have surrendered their God-ordained purpose is they are just too busy. Some will give God a couple hours on Sunday morning, but they are just too tired to attempt to dive into a project that demands time and effort.

Unfortunately, some people give up their God assignments because it doesn't happen right away. They usually don't pay attention to the subtle promptings of the Holy Spirit as He tries to inspire them. Many people haven't accessed tools that are available to help them. They haven't taken classes on how to do what God as asked them to do. Whether it's writing a book, composing a song, starting a business or ministry, they haven't educated themselves on how to do it with proficiency. They assume the content, business plan, or organization structure is just going to flow out of them naturally and that may not be the case. Oftentimes, there are steps that need to be taken before the assignment can be borne through you. So many people have given up before they have started.

When God gives someone a God assignment, He usually doesn't tell the person how and when it will happen. It is in our human nature to make assumptions about the *how* and *when*. Then, when things don't materialize when we expect it, most people give up. They added their fantasies and assumptions to the word God gave them and they give up when it didn't happen the way they expected.

Another thing that can cause someone to give up on their destiny promises is disappointment. I understand it. I have been there. We can go through losses and heartache where we feel so disappointed that we lack the motivation to shine for God. Maybe our loved one we thought was going to be healed passed away. Maybe our husband or wife left us. Maybe our child is on drugs, and we thought God was going to deliver them. Our life isn't what we thought it would be when we gave God our "yes." Our disappointments have caused us to enter a setback season, so our assignments get placed on hold and are often aborted all together.

I'm a Lost Cause

There are some people that have embraced the sub-conscious programming line that says, "I'm a lost cause." They may not admit it to their family and friends. And they may not consciously be aware of it. But it shows up in their actions and comments. They don't try because they believe they can't. They don't attempt to believe God for miracles because they believe God won't give them one. They won't attempt any God assignments because they have embraced the lie that it wasn't for them. They cling to lies like, they didn't hear God correctly, or they are not talented or holy enough. They agree with their negative self-talk, and they are just biding their time until it's time for them to pass. They would rather live in defeat than believe for more. It's easier for them.

Conclusion

Millions of people have surrendered to their carnal nature. They don't even attempt to live a godly lifestyle. They have rationalized that they aren't that bad, and they will still get into heaven, so why even try. While others live in defeat because they won't attempt to use their faith to obtain the promises that are available to them through the Word. Their ignorance and comfort zones keep them broke, sick, and in mental distress. And still others have given up on their God assignments because of busyness and disappointments. Millions have embraced a passive posture. They have no fight in them.

Have you given up on trying? Is it possible that you have a subconscious mindset that says, "I give up?" If so, ask God to help you. Take that area of sin, or disappointment and lay it at the foot of the cross. Ask for forgiveness and ask God to show you how to pick up the sword again. You aren't done on this planet until God calls you home. If there is still breath in your lungs, there is still a chance to fight for what you know to be true.

Galatians 6:9 says, *"And let us not grow weary while doing good, for in due season we shall reap if we do not lose heart."* If you have lost heart, ask God to repair the nooks and crannies that are filled with disappointment and try again. God has got you. He is the God of the second chances. Try again.

Chapter 8

The Shame Ditch

People have secrets. Almost everyone has things in their past that they are ashamed of. It could be a big secret that would change the opinions of others towards us. Or we could carry a painful and private memory of when someone hurt us.

Certainly, every detail of our lives is not everyone's business. However, this chapter discusses those areas of shame that impact a person's emotional well-being.

A large percentage of people carry guilt, condemnation, and shame that affects their success in life.

The secret can be anything. Maybe you stole something. Perhaps you had an abortion or convinced someone else to have one. You could have been physically, emotionally, or sexually abusive at one time in your life. You may have gotten drunk and hit someone with your car. Maybe you gossiped and caused someone to get fired. Or you could have hurt someone in a different way. It can be any number of things.

Whatever that incident was, it is common for a person to consider themselves as either the victim or the villain. It is even more common for a person to feel like they are both.

Years ago, when I attended a large church, I was an altar worker. A young woman came forward for prayer. As we sat in the back counseling room, she told me about a very traumatic experience she had as a child. She said she watched old Westerns and one day she decided to play cowboy. She was in her backyard with her dad and her dog while her dad did yard work. She decided to get on top of the shed because she was going to do what she saw the cowboys do. Cowboys jumped off the roof and onto their horses and road away. Well, she jumped from the shed onto the dog, and it broke the dog's leg.

The father screamed at his little girl and said it was her fault that he had to kill the dog to "put it out of its misery." He took a knife and slit the dog's throat in front of her. He then forced the girl's face into the blood and rubbed her nose in it (like she was a dog that pooped where it shouldn't have).

Admittedly, that is one of the worst things I have ever heard of a father doing. He didn't have to kill the dog, and he certainly didn't have to traumatize the girl by rubbing her face in the blood. She was absolutely a victim of bad parenting. But she also felt guilty because she jumped off the roof and broke the dog's leg. She felt like both a victim and a villain.

She carried that guilt and shame into her adult life. As she shared her story, she also told me that she had been cutting herself. She had been punishing herself by taking a razer and making herself bleed.

I recognize that this is a very traumatizing experience and most of us haven't experienced anything near that. However, it is very possible that we are punishing ourselves over experiences in our past. We may not be doing it with a razor, but we could still be thinking and acting in a way that harms ourselves. We could be in a ditch in life because there is a subconscious limitation in us that won't allow our success. We could be sabotaging ourselves because of secret shame that is hiding in a crevasse of our heart. We may sabotage opportunities for success because we feel unworthy. We may be staying in an abusive relationship because we don't feel like we deserve better. Or we may stay distant from God because we don't think He can forgive us when we can't forgive ourselves.

My Shame

Some of you know my history, but I will give a recap of a section of it. I was raised in a conservative Christian home but backslid when I was 19 years old and stayed backslidden for ten years.

In June of 1994, I was at rock bottom. I was devastated over a breakup with a boyfriend. My best friend had moved out of state. A year and a half earlier, an ex-boyfriend committed suicide when I didn't reconcile with him. He shot himself through the heart exactly two years to the day that we had started dating. I had been a division manager at a Fortune 500 company that got reorganized while I was on a business trip. I gave my blood, sweat, and tears to a job only to be *stabbed in the back* by another manager that wanted my position. With my departure, I lost all the friendships that I had at that company.

I was done. I had nothing. I felt like life had taken a baseball bat and knocked me to the ground. In June of 1994, after crying for three days straight, I surrendered my heart back to God. My life was a mess, I failed. I needed God.

I started attending a Vineyard Church. I remember I basically cried the entire service every time I was there, until one day in August. One Sunday afternoon, I woke up from a nap and I heard the Holy Spirit say, "go, get baptized." I looked in the bulletin from that morning and I saw that there was a baptism happening that afternoon. So, I quickly grabbed a change of clothes and went to get baptized.

That evening, at the Sunday night service, the pastor had those that had been baptized come forward for prayer. I was *slain in the spirit,* meaning the power of God hit me and I ended up laying on the ground. I was vaguely aware that music was playing, and people were standing around me praying for me. As I lay there, I saw colorful laser lights shoot across the inside of my eyelids.

A couple days later, I asked God about the laser-colored lights. The Holy Spirit said, "I was doing laser surgery on your heart." I then realized that my emotional trauma was healed. Things that used to hurt didn't hurt anymore. I didn't go around crying all the time. I could still remember the events of my past, but the emotional pain was gone.

A couple weeks after that, I found myself enrolled in a Bible school and my life was completely different. So much happened in that Bible school, both good and bad, but I am not going to take the time to go into detail now about it.

In July of 1995, I was at a women's retreat organized by a new church that I had started attending. That Saturday morning before starting my day, I had read Isaiah 42. After lunch, we were told to get alone with God and have some private time.

I took my Bible, and I walked over to the outdoor amphitheater. I decided to reread Isaiah 42 again. I read through verse 5, and then something happened.

I had an angelic encounter. I looked up from my Bible and a pure white hummingbird was hovering a foot away from my face. It wasn't a regular hummingbird. Beams of light were radiating from it and its face had humanistic qualities. It looked like it was a special effect from a movie. The humanlike face had expressions of love and kindness. I realized this was an angelic encounter. Then, I heard in my spirit, "Be encouraged." The creature gave me a knowing look, then flew away.

I was a bit stunned after that happened, but I sensed that I was supposed to continue reading out of Isaiah 42. When I read verses 6 and 7, I was almost overcome with emotion. It was as if I understood those two verses were a word from God to me. We know the passage is prophetically talking about Jesus, but the Holy Spirit emphasized to me that it is also my commission.

Isaiah 42:6-7 reads, *"I, the Lord, have called you in righteousness, and I will hold your hand; I will keep you and give you as a covenant to the people, as a light to the Gentiles, to open blind eyes, to bring out prisoners from the prison, those who sit in darkness from the prison house."*

Those verses contained details of my calling from God. I am called to help bring illumination to those that are spiritually blind. God wants me to help those that are imprisoned by shame, depression, fear, pride, and other soul bondages.

I could write paragraphs about these two verses but there are a couple aspects I want to focus on. When the verse said, *"I will keep you and give as a covenant to the people."* The Holy Spirit conveyed the verse in a way that let me know that He was going *keep* me by protecting and preserving me. I knew I would have a season of being hidden while He preserved me. That may be why I have never promoted my books or why I never did any self-promotion for speaking events. I didn't know how long my hidden season would last. But I knew that when God did fully release me, my testimony was supposed to be an example to others. I am supposed to be transparent and share details of my life.

There were other times when the Holy Spirit communicated this to me as well. In the summer of 1996, my friend Betty and I got in my car about to leave an all-day Christian conference we had attended. Back then, it was the style to wear big earrings, but they hurt our pierced ears. As we waited for our turn to exit the parking garage, I took off an earring. As I did, it looked like the metal post that goes through my ear had broken off and was attached to the butterfly back. But when we looked at the front of the earring, the post was still there. There were two posts! Betty and I couldn't figure out what we were looking at. After I dropped her off at her apartment, I asked the Holy

Spirit about it. The Holy Spirit said, "The things that have pierced you, I will heal in others."

So, that experience was another confirmation that I am supposed to share details of my life in the books that I write. God was going to use my experiences to demonstrate His grace.

When the verse said, *I will give you as a covenant*, I knew what it meant. God will use me as an example to confirm His promises to His people. The word *covenant* means agreement, contract, promise, pledge, or bond. God was wanting to use my traumas and dramas to pledge to others that what He did for me, He will do for them.

Hey, God supernaturally healed my broken heart when I was laid out on the floor, and I saw colored laser lights on the inside of my eyelids. I will gladly be an example of what God can and will do in the future with emotional healing. I could talk about the emotional trauma of being molested as a child by my eldest brother. I could talk about the suicide of my boyfriend and how his sister got up at his funeral and blamed me. I could talk about all kinds of rejections and hurt. But I didn't want to talk about abortion.

I knew God was telling me I had to tell people about the abortions I had. I didn't want to. I wanted to keep my shame hidden.

In the mid 80's, when I had my first abortion, my parents didn't even know I had a boyfriend or that I was sleeping with him. Fear of shame from family, friends, and old church people, plus the fact that my boyfriend demanded that I get an abortion, were what drove the decision.

I, like many girls in that position, compartmentalized the event. I didn't allow myself to think about it. I didn't emotionally process what I was doing. I just brushed it *under the rug* and stored it in a crevasse of my heart that I didn't go near. So, naturally, when I found myself pregnant again, I did the same thing without even giving it much thought. It got locked away in a hidden room in my heart to be forever my secret that no one was supposed to ever know about.

Back then, I didn't want to share my secret with anyone. I didn't want to be a Christian *poster child* for abortion. At the time, in 1995, there was only one woman on Christian TV that admitted to having an abortion. And every time she spoke about it, she appeared to have to repent all over again, trying to get the viewers' approval. It was almost as if she felt the viewers scorn and she was begging for forgiveness from them. She didn't demonstrate a woman that walked in righteousness. She acted like and was treated like a woman that would forever carry the shame of the actions she took in her youth.

Isaiah 42:6 says, *"I, the Lord, have called you in righteousness."* This sentence still brings tears to my eyes. God sent an angel to tell me I was righteous! In July of 1995, I had my last abortion only two and a half years earlier with the boyfriend that committed suicide. What? God was calling me righteous?!?! Sure, I felt righteous about most stuff but deep down in me, where the shame of abortion hid, I wasn't righteous.

Shortly after that, I recognized that I needed to emotionally process the abortion issue. Up to that point, I guess I thought everything was okay with me. My past was covered by the redemptive work of the cross. I was done with that chapter of my life.

However, I began to recognize that while God healed the emotional pain I had the year prior, I had never submitted the abortion thing to God. It was tucked away in a dark corner of my heart. I never asked for forgiveness or (metaphorically) laid that burden down at the foot of the cross. After that angelic encounter, I recognized that I wasn't allowed to keep my private shame. I understood that God wanted to use my testimony of His forgiveness in that area to help others that keep that same secret.

Peel the Onion

When I got back from that women's retreat, I went into a season where I made myself recount the details of my abortions. I made myself remember and I journalized. I wrote down what I could remember about the fears and the details of my life at the time. I repented for my actions, and I mourned the loss of my babies. It wasn't a comfortable season, but it was a necessary one. I took time to peel away the layers of the onion so

I could understand and emotionally process that area of my life.

This may surprise you, but when I set aside time to deal with the abortions in my life, I wasn't entirely sure how many I had had. After the first one, I went into an autopilot behavior when I got pregnant again and I didn't allow myself to think about it.

I lived with my first long-term boyfriend for five and a half years and I discovered that I had four abortions with him. And as mentioned, I also had an abortion with the boyfriend that committed suicide. So, five of my children are in heaven.

God is so kind. In that season, God gave me two visions of heaven where He allowed me to see my kids. In the first vision, I saw a little girl with long wavy brown hair. She was smiling and waving at me. She looked to be about 8 or 9 years old, which would have been her age had she been born full term. Then I saw a little boy who appeared to be about five years old. I am guessing he was my youngest. He had a mischievous grin on his face as he waved at me. You know, it is funny, while I dated that first long-term boyfriend, I could never imagine what our kids would have looked like. But God, in his goodness, showed me two of them. And they were expressing love and kindness towards me. They weren't mad at me.

Then, at a different time while I was still emotionally processing my abortions, I had a vision of Fred, my boyfriend that committed suicide, playing kickball with his toe-headed toddler son. Fred never wanted kids because he was abused as a child and didn't want to bring any children into an evil world. But there he was, enjoying fatherhood to the fullest. I can still hear both Fred and the little boy's laughter in my memory of that day I saw them in heaven playing.

What does it mean to *peel the onion,* to emotionally process an event in your life?

1) Give it to God. We need to repent. We need to lift the rug that we swept our secret under and bring it out into the light. Why are we hiding something from God when He sees it all? We need to acknowledge our wrongdoing. Absolutely other people influenced our decision, but we still need to take responsibility for the role we played.

2) Remember and Examine. It was a different time back then. I remember a week after my first abortion; my best friend told me she was pregnant. I never told her about my pregnancy and abortion. My friend carried the baby full term and gave the baby up for adoption. Her family scorned and shamed her the entire time she was pregnant and even after that. Her family didn't allow her to go to family gatherings. Her family balled her out for bringing shame to the family. They forced her to move out of state to a Catholic Unwed Mother's home that specialized in private adoptions.

As I journaled, I remembered the mental torment I faced when I had that first abortion. In 1995, I had so much more spiritual knowledge than I did in 1986.

That year of Bible school taught me so much about the spirit world. I recognized that demons tormented my mind in 1986 when I was pregnant. I didn't just have normal fears. The demonic mental attacks literally made me feel like I didn't have a choice. The fears of:

"My boyfriend will leave me."

"I will lose my job."

"No one will hire a pregnant woman."

"I won't be able to work if I have a baby."

"I will bring shame to the family.

"My family will forever change their opinion of me."

"I won't have money to survive."

"I will be homeless."

"I won't be able to care for a baby."

There was so much fear attacking my mind. There was rationalizing and reasoning thoughts as well, like: "It's bad timing. You can have a baby later when you have a husband and have money. You can't provide a home for a child right now."

Not only do young girls facing pregnancy have unbearable fears attacking their mind, they also have an identity crisis. Their identity sometimes has a hard time accepting the change into motherhood. They don't see themselves as a mother, so the prospect of motherhood feels very wrong. It is not who they are, so they reject it.

Part of emotionally processing an event is reflecting on the mindset you were in at the time you made your decision. What factors influenced you? Every situation is like a diamond. It's multifaceted. There are different sides, aspects, and factors that influence a situation.

A big determining factor in my abortions was the response of my boyfriends. That first long-term boyfriend was adamant that we needed to have the abortions. There was no wiggle room or debate. He was firm that it was both of our decisions because it affected both of us for the rest of our lives. The second boyfriend was softer in his approach, but he had the same view. He felt he was too messed up emotionally to be a father.

It's important to make yourself see the issue or incident from different angles. If you don't, it is too easy to view yourself or others involved as either the victim or the villain. When the reality of the situation is, most people involved are both the victim and the villain. Things are not black or white; there are shades of gray when you view your past from different angles and perspectives.

3) Mourn the Loss. Those weeks that I took to examine the issue of abortion in my life were difficult emotionally. I cried a lot. The crying wasn't continual repenting to God. God is quick to forgive when we submit the issue to Him. I was crying because I was mourning the loss of my children.

I am sure the reason I repeated the behavior and had subsequent abortions after the first one was, I had never emotionally processed the gravity of my actions.

I didn't allow myself to consider that it was my child, not just a blob of cells forming an embryo.

4) Forgive Yourself. I have known women that have never forgiven themselves for the abortions they had in their youth. As a result, they haven't allowed themselves to succeed or even enjoy their life. They carry a yoke on their shoulders. They believe they aren't worthy of forgiveness, love, and acceptance because they don't forgive, love, or accept themselves.

When the Holy Spirit highlighted Isaiah 42:6 where it says, *"I have called you in righteousness,"* it struck through my heart. God saw that hidden corner of shame and He called me righteous. He labeled me forgiven.

Righteous means right standing with God. It means just as if I had never sinned. It means the slate was wiped clean. I don't have to wear a scarlet letter on my chest for the rest of my life. I didn't have to carry shame, condemnation, and regret. People may still condemn me when they hear my story, but God doesn't. I don't have to walk with *my tail between my legs* like a fearful dog. God calls me righteous. God pronounced me free from my past mistakes.

We must forgive ourselves. The Bible says in Matt 6:14 we must forgive others or God won't forgive us. Healing and forgiveness are linked. We must forgive others and forgive ourselves because if we don't it will block physical and emotional healing.

5) Tell Your Story. Part of breaking shame is blowing up the secrecy around it. For me, when I was emotionally processing the abortion thing, God made me tell others my secret. It was very hard.

I didn't want to tell my parents. I didn't want to do it in person or on the phone. I ended up writing a letter and faxing it to them at their home office. A couple hours later, I received a voicemail from my mother that was very loving and accepting.

Next, I felt like God wanted me to tell my sister, Cindy. Cindy had five kids, and she was an advocate for the prolife movement. I thought for sure I was going to get condemnation from her, but she was very loving and gracious. She didn't have any hostility or condemnation in her words or tone in my call with her. She was just as gracious as my mom was.

The surprise reaction was from my best friend at the time. I told her at a coffee shop when we were having breakfast one morning. She told me later that afternoon that hearing about my abortions filled her with rage. She said she wanted to reach across the table and rip my limbs from my shoulders because that is what I did when I allowed the doctors to abort my babies.

We can't be held a prisoner of our secrets if we expose our secrets. Ask God for wisdom in how and when you do it. But there is a sense of freedom when we release the toxic shame we are holding. The timing is important. We should make sure we have finished *peeling the onion* before we do the last step of breaking our silence. We have to have the issue settled within us before we share it with others because not everyone will necessarily be gracious with their reaction. When we have reconciled the issue with God, the reactions of others won't matter.

It's Your Turn

I just shared an area of secret shame I had in the 90s. Is there something that you have locked away in a secret place in your heart? If so, have ever emotionally processed it? Have you repented to God and *laid it at the foot of the cross?* Have you forced yourself to remember the details? Have you examined the incident from all angles? Have you asked God to show you insights that you didn't know before?

If you aren't sure if you carry secret shame or not, there is a way to tell. If you have not emotionally processed something from your past, you either: 1) don't talk about it, or 2) don't stop talking about it.

In the case of abortion, it was my secret. I didn't talk about it and I didn't emotionally process it until 1995. An example of the latter was when my boyfriend of two years committed suicide. After his death, I used to sit in bars and tell everyone who would listen about it. I was hurting so I talked about it often, even to strangers. That was a sign that the emotional wound was still fresh. But thankfully, God supernaturally healed that pain in August of 1994.

God is the healer of hearts. Isaiah 54:4 says, *"Do not fear, for you will not be ashamed; neither be disgraced, for you will not be put to shame. For you will forget the shame of your youth, and not remember the reproach of your widowhood anymore."* God will help you break the chains you are carrying if you release your pain and shame to Him.

Chapter 9

Our New Identity

We were all born with a carnal, Adamic nature. When mankind fell in the garden, pride was sired into the bloodline of man. Lucifer fell because of pride. When Adam and Eve, disobeyed God, it gave authority of the Earth to Lucifer and allowed pride and carnality to rein in the hearts of mankind.

Pride is the primary soul iniquity, but people have other *diseases of the soul* as well. As mentioned in the first chapter, there are twelve *diseases of the soul.* They are propensities towards certain categories of sin and they can act like a cancer in our subconscious mind.

In addition to soul iniquities, we can also have counterproductive, negative, autopilot thoughts or behaviors that kick in when they are triggered by situations in our lives, as discussed in the second chapter. These glitches (wrinkles, lines of programming) in our subconscious mind feel normal to us. They can be manifestations of our soul iniquities, or they can be other programming codes we embraced from our childhood, our experiences, our culture, our friends, our mental reasoning, or even demonic suggestions. They are learned behaviors and if we don't correct them at their origin, they can become a pattern for us. If they are not corrected, they can transition from a random thought or action into a lifestyle pattern. If they don't get corrected, it is usually because they aren't recognized. Since most people don't take their thoughts captive as the Bible instructs us to in 2 Cor. 10:5, they *fly under our radar.*

Just like our autopilot glitches can sneak by undetected, so can the ditch mindsets that have been discussed in this book. We don't realize we are obeying our comfort zones or identity-shaping words. We may not even know we are depressed and if we do, we think it is normal because negative circumstances may be happening. We don't give our blame-shifting a second thought because it's easier to point the finger at someone else than take responsibility for our mistakes. We often don't recognize that we have embraced a give-up attitude and if we do, we feel justified because we are tired of trying. And finally, those of us carrying secret shame are so used to living with our chains, we don't realize that we are in bondage.

The six ditches discussed in this small book can absolutely make the difference between success and failure. They are not too big to fix. They are ditches, they are not deep pits. It may be difficult to get out of but it's possible. Sure, it seems like when you get your footing, the loose gravel slips, and you end up *back at square one*. But if you keep trying, you will eventually get out. It takes effort to get out of a ditch, and it will take effort to change wrong mindsets.

I do think these wrong mindsets are easier to break than uprooting a soul iniquity, but they are corrected the same way. First, we need to recognize and acknowledge them in our behavior. Then, we need to understand their harm. Reflect on how it has affected your life. Recognizing the characteristics of a ditch within yourself is really half the battle. Like with *diseases of the soul*, understanding how they manifest helps you see it in your behavior in real time.

Our Christian walk isn't about being perfect. We aren't going to be perfect this side of heaven because we have a carnal nature. However, we can walk in levels of freedom that we didn't know were possible. Will we always have some levels of residual pride? Yes, but we can root out big chunks of it. We can allow the Holy Spirit to do His surgery on us and cut away most of the large tumors that are harming our life.

When the Bible talks about renewing our mind (Rom 12:2), it doesn't just mean we are supposed to memorize a few scriptures. Renewing our mind involves educating ourselves and uprooting negative beliefs and behaviors. We are getting the right stuff in us and getting the wrong stuff out of us. We can recognize the wrong stuff by doing 2 Cor. 10:5. We take every thought captive and challenge the thoughts that don't line up with the word of God.

We need to receive good identity-shaping words and the promises of God until it changes our identity. As a reminder, our conscious mind is the gateway to our subconscious mind. We need to hear, receive, repeat, rehearse, and meditate on the word of God, both the logos word (the written word, Bible passages) and the Rhema word (the spoken word, those things the Holy Spirit whispers to us).

We Are Loved

As we learn to renew our mind, by rooting out wrong thinking and developing right thinking, there are three things we need to focus on. The first thing is a greater understanding that we are loved by God.

I have known Christians that haven't received the revelation that God loves them. They know the Bible says that God loves mankind but, in their heart, they don't believe God loves them individually.

One friend comes to mind. We were having a discussion, and she was sad that a man that she liked hadn't taken a romantic interest in her. I told her, "God adores you."

She said, "I don't think He does."

Surprised, I asked why she thought that.

She said, "If God loved me, He would answer my questions I have asked Him. He wouldn't be denying me having a husband and kids."

I then spoke to her about the timing of God not always being our timing. I told her there are normally things God needs to do in us and in the other person before we are ready for marriage.

But that night, I had an insight that I had never thought of before. Knowing that God loves us is like any other type of faith. In order for us to have faith for healing, we have to get the healing promise from our head to our heart. The same is true with knowing that God loves us. We need to get that information from our head to our heart, from our conscious mind to our subconscious mind. We are responsible for taking the word of God that He loves us and meditating on it until it sinks down into our heart.

In her mind, God had to prove His love for her by giving her the desires of her heart. Because she didn't get married and have kids when she wanted, that was proof to her that God didn't care about her. She wanted to see it, before she would believes it. That is the problem. A person with that mindset won't understand God's love for them. Like with most supernatural things, you have to believe it, before you see it. Not the other way around. If she believed that God loved her in her gut, she would start to see all kinds of confirmations of that.

A sign of God's love isn't that we get everything we want in the timing we want. I'm sorry to say, but that is immature thinking. It's like a four-year-old crying because a parent didn't let them have ice cream for dinner.

Understanding God's love is trusting Him to know who is the right person for us and trusting that His timing is perfect. We can actually sabotage and delay our lives if we accept and embrace wrong mindsets like God doesn't love us because I am not getting my way. We need to trust that if God isn't bringing the right person to us right now, then there are things in them or in us that need to be worked out first. We don't want toxic or premature relationships. We are all a work in progress, and we all have things that should get worked out of us before we are ready for certain blessings and promises.

When we know in our gut that God loves us, we won't be as desperate to get the love and attention of a potential boyfriend or girlfriend. We will have confidence in ourselves and in God. We won't tolerate manipulative or abusive behavior because we are not emotionally needy and *thirsty* for affection.

When we know God loves us and has our best interest at heart, we won't be jealous of friends that get married or have kids before us. Our love walk with God will be so rich that we won't even be tempted to look over the fence to see if the *grass is greener* over there.

Matthew 6:33 says, *"But seek first the kingdom of God and His righteousness, and all these things shall be added to you."* Our job is to seek God with all our heart. That attention that you want to pour out on a spouse or child, dedicate that attention to God. Go on dates with the Holy Spirit. Spend quality time with Him. Develop your love relationship with Him, then God will bring the other relationships into your life.

We Are Righteous

The second thing we need to get down into our gut is that we are righteous. This seems like such a basic tenant of faith in Christianity, but I am surprised how many people do not understand it. Years ago, I knew a pastor that had a *works mentality*. He was constantly striving for holiness (which was good) but he also placed too much holiness expectations on his congregation. Of course, it is the pastor's job to preach holiness but his push was too strong and his congregation numbers quickly decreased. We can't earn God's love and righteousness. It is a free gift. Humans are going to struggle with their carnal nature so they need grace in the journey. I also had a roommate that was raised Catholic who also didn't have the righteous revelation in her heart. There were still traces of the Catholic ideology in her that says "you get into heaven by your works."

Back in chapter one I talked about agreeing with a sermon in our mind but not downloading it into our subconscious mind. I compared the human psyche to a computer. Both of the people mentioned in the above paragraph, the pastor and the woman who was raised Catholic, attended the same spirit-filled Bible college as me in the 90's. They had the same class on righteousness that I had. But that teaching was just head knowledge, and it didn't sink down into their subconscious mind.

Roman's 5:19 is so insightful. It reads, *"For as by one man's disobedience many were made sinners, so also by one Man's obedience many were made righteous."* I referenced at the beginning of this chapter that pride was sired into humanity at the fall of Adam. Through Adam, carnality was born in us and our nature became corrupted. But through the obedience of Jesus, our nature has become righteous.

Does that mean we no longer have an Adamic carnal nature? No. But it means that God the Father sees us through the redemptive work of Christ, so He sees us as righteous, holy, and pure. 2 Corinthians 5:21 says,

"For He made Him who knew no sin to be sin for us, that we might become the righteousness of God in Him."

We can lay aside all addictions and outwardly sins, but we are never going to be perfect this side of heaven. There will be times when our Adamic nature will try to flare up. It may not happen very often, but there may be times when we want to cuss at another driver who cut us off. Or we may be tempted to vent to our friend when someone slandered us. Or maybe carnality will rise and we tell a *white lie.* We all have carnality in us. Yes, we can reduce it but there will be times when our imperfections manifest.

God's love for us isn't based on our perfection and discipline. Our righteousness is a gift that comes from our position of being a child of God. It can't be earned. It's not about our performance.

If the concept of righteousness is head knowledge and not heart knowledge, I encourage you to meditate on the verses that talk about it. Work on getting that Biblical concept to sink down from your head to your heart.

We Are Victorious

I see so many believers that live their lives as victims. They may not have a traditional *victim mentality* that was discussed in chapter Five, but they certainly aren't victorious. So many believers have a persona that exudes fear and defeat. Like ten of the tribes of Israel, they have a *grasshopper mentality*.

I am especially surprised by how many Christians are afraid of demons. A woman called me and wanted encouragement and counsel. She talked about demons tormenting her, so I started to advise her on the believer's authority. She didn't want to hear it. She wanted me to just say a prayer of encouragement over her. I told her that demons thrive in <u>fear</u> and <u>ignorance</u> and it's important to dispel both of those things so the demonic attacks would lose their power. She didn't want me that talk about that. She believed that the more spiritual knowledge she had, the more the demons would attack her. I tried to tell her it was just the opposite. The more fear and ignorance we have, the bigger the target we are for the kingdom of darkness.

Another reason why so many Christians live in fear is they lack an understanding of what faith is. Most haven't understood that the trajectory of their life is set by the faith that resides in their subconscious mind. If they have authentic faith in God's promises, their life will reap blessings and peace. If they have faith in their fears, negative things will follow them. Faith is believing something in your subconscious mind. People that have a lot of fear believe negative things will happen to them. And as a result, negative things follow them.

There is a spiritual element to it and a psychological one. We know that the spirit world operates by agreement. When we speak God's word over our situations, it releases angels to work on our behalf. Likewise, if we agree with and verbalize our fears, we authorize demons to wreak havoc in our circumstances. Our words authorize the spirit realm either for good or bad.

On the psychological front, if we expect favor and respect from others, we usually get it. We put out a vibe that others pick up on. If we don't respect ourselves, others won't respect us.

Most Christians live below their station in life because they lack spiritual maturity. Most believers don't have a full understanding of what it means to be a child of God.

Galatians 1:1-7 reads, *"Now I say that the heir, as long as he is a child, does not differ at all from a slave, though he is master of all, 2) but is under guardians and stewards until the time appointed by the father. 3) Even so we, when we were children, were in bondage under the elements of the world, 4) But when the fullness of time had come, God sent forth His Son, born of a woman, born under the law. 5) to redeem those who were under the law, that we might receive the adoption as sons. 6) And because you are sons, God has sent forth the Spirit of His Son into your hearts, crying out, "Abba Father!" 7) Therefore you are no longer a slave but a son, and if a son then an heir of God through Christ."*

As the passage tells us, most of God's kids walk around like servants. We are willing to take the scraps because, unfortunately, we don't think we deserve better. We think we are being godly by expressing humility and having a servant's heart. Yes, we need to have those things, but we also need to have a knowing in our gut that we are a child of God. Our identity needs to embrace the inheritance that God has for us. With spiritual maturity, we should carry the family traits. The DNA of God dwells in us, we should be bold about commanding the storm to cease in Jesus' name as the Holy Spirit leads. We should walk with confidence knowing our spiritual authority and inheritance. As the Galatians passage says, we are sons and when we mature, we shouldn't still act like servants. Jesus made us His disciples, His ambassadors. Yet, most Christians don't act the way Jesus acted. We don't access the angels assigned to us to "right" the wrongs that we see in the world. We don't reach out to help others.

I believe this Galatians passage is prophetic. It says, "until the time appointed by the Father," and "in the fullness of time." I believe we are the generation that will usher in the return of Jesus. I believe we are the people that are on the Earth for the appointed time of the Father. We are stepping into the fullness of time, and as such, we will embody a more victorious persona. We won't walk with our head bowed down in shame, fear, or defeat. We will walk as sons and daughters of the King of Kings.

Renew Our Minds

I believe we are the generation that will have a greater revelation of the love that God has for us individually as we renew our minds. We will have a knowing in our gut that we were made righteous by Jesus' obedience on the cross. And I believe we are the people that will finally walk in the authority as sons and daughters of the God Most High.

As we renew our minds to the word of God, it will transform our identity. It will change the way we view ourselves. At the end of each of the ditch chapters, I gave some helpful hints on how to break those wrong cycles. Those suggestions, coupled with understanding God's love, our righteousness through Him, and the victory and authority that is available to us, truly can change us. We can become the people God created us to be. We can step into our potential and live in victory.

www.ingramcontent.com/pod-product-compliance
Lightning Source LLC
Chambersburg PA
CBHW071311130626
46556CB00004B/1572